THE COMING BANKING HOLIDAY

How It Will Happen, and Why You Should Get Your Savings, Investments, IRAs, and Gold Overseas Now (While You Still Can)

JOHN & MONICA MILLER

As Vice President Joe Biden admitted in June 2009, *"Literally one of the early [discussions was]* **whether we might have to call a bank holiday…a bank holiday on the day after we were sworn in.***"*

—Gerald Celente, *Winter Trend's Journal*

This is our story—how a middle-class couple, living in Hawaii, moved their savings, and investments to New Zealand and Australia, in anticipation of probable US dollar devaluation. This book was written to help other concerned Americans living in the US, to do the same, before the "banking holiday" happens.

—John and Monica Miller

Copyright © 2012 by John & Monica Miller

All rights reserved. No portion of this book may be reproduced mechanically, electronically, or by any other means, including photocopying, without written permission of the publisher. It is illegal to copy this book, post it to a website, or distribute it by any other means without permission from the publisher.

John and Monica Miller
Waiheke Island, Auckland, New Zealand
Maui, Hawaii
(727) 564–9416
John@Banking-Holiday.com
www.Banking-Holiday.com

Limits of Liability and Disclaimer of Warranty

The author and publisher shall not be liable for your misuse of this material. This book is strictly for informational and educational purposes.

Warning—Disclaimer

The purpose of this book is to educate and entertain. The author and/or publisher do not guarantee that anyone following these techniques, suggestions, tips, ideas, or strategies will become successful. The author and/or publisher shall have neither liability nor responsibility to anyone with respect to any loss or damage caused, or alleged to be caused, directly or indirectly by the information contained in this book.

Interest rates quoted in this book were based on April 2012 data, and are subject to change. Call the authors for current rates at: (727) 564-9416, or e-mail them at: John@Banking-Holiday.com.

ISBN: 978-0-9853373-0-8

To find out more about bringing some, or all of your savings and investments to NZ, please visit our website: www.banking-holiday.com. There, you'll find continuously updated information on events leading to the banking holiday, reporting, law changes, and recommendations for how to legally get your money and investments overseas. This book will point out what a "banking holiday" is, the history of banking holidays in the US, what the current administration is saying about them, and what you can do about it.

Some of the finest financial writers and forecasters have made this book possible. At the end of each chapter, Monica and I wrote a few paragraphs concerning how we approached each problem and offered our opinions.

For those readers or radio listeners needing some assistance in getting your savings and investments out of harm's way, please e-mail us at John@Banking-Holiday.com. Monica and I will do our best to answer all of your questions and concerns.

There is now no need for you to travel to NZ to open a savings, or investment account, as we did. This can all be done for you easily and safely using the Internet or fax. The minimum size ("custodian account") is only $25,000. This could be made up from a combination of savings and investments. For example, $12,500 could be used to purchase a one-month Australian CD (they call it a "term deposit"). Presently this savings program is paying 4.3% interest. The other $12,500 could be placed in a few strong natural resource stocks. If you'd like more information on how to open a custodian account, please call us at (727) 564–9416 (US phone number) or e-mail us at John@Banking-Holiday.com.

For those wishing to buy small amounts of silver in the US, Dave Morgan, considered the number-one silver expert, highly recommends "Silver Saver" (silversaver.com/share/5FXFR). Here's what he said in his March, 2012 newsletter: "I have known one of the founders personally for years and will assert this program is run with the highest integrity. I participate myself."

A few hundred dollars each month is deducted from your checking account (painless). When your account reaches a couple of thousand, you should ask "silver saver" to send you your silver coins.

—John Miller

TESTIMONIALS

"John, overall your book seems to have a lot of valuable and helpful information. You bring up facts that are often not discussed in the mainstream."

—Deborah P., Maui, Hawaii

"There are so many of these type books now on the market today, such as Currency Wars, *and I've read most of them; this one ranks right up there!"*

—Bill Templeton, Auckland, New Zealand

"Great guidebook for the middle class about to lose their retirement savings; it tells exactly what is about to occur and what they can do about it."

—Becki Williams, Orlando, Florida

*"If you liked '*Currency Wars,*' the #1 best seller, you're going to love* The Coming Banking Holiday*!"*

—John Sellers, Tampa, Florida

ACKNOWLEDGMENTS

This book is dedicated to the thousands of investment club members that have stayed with us, learned with us, and survived financially with us, over the past 25 years.

Our thanks, especially, to members of our original investment club: the Tampa Bay Investment Club. The Tampa club was featured in *Money* magazine, and was said to be one of the largest and most successful investment clubs in the US.

Further thanks go to the members of the Maui Investment Club, an educational, social investment club located on the beautiful island of Maui, Hawaii. Without their support, the current Investment Club International would not have been born, and our journey to NZ would never have taken place. It was their financial questions that encouraged us to visit NZ in 2008, in search of answers. We came back only once to say our goodbyes. We soon hope to be permanent residents of NZ, but will, of course, maintain our US citizenship.

This book is further dedicated to our good friend, Phil Bayly. If it weren't for Phil, we'd still be living in Clearwater, Florida, watching our house and stock market investments fall in value, while the "be happy" folks at CNBC were saying that "all is well"! Well, all wasn't well. Phil explained to us that the general stock market is rigged and has been for the last hundred years. He explained that although they can rig precious metals, and precious metal stocks in the short run, they can't in the long run.

Due to Phil's advice, we cashed it all in, in 2005, visited our local bullion dealer, and said: "What's a Maple Leaf and how much do they cost?" He said $350. The rest is history. Gold, as we write this book, is $1,775.

We'd like to especially thank the following investment professionals for assisting in this endeavor, for without them, this book could not be possible:

Gerald Celente (TrendsResearch.com)

Porter Stansberry (StansberryResearch.com)

Simon Black (SovereignMan.com)

Jim Sinclair (JSMineset.com)

Dr. Steve Sjuggerud (DailyWealth.com)

John Williams (ShadowStats.com)

David McAlvany (McAlvanyWeeklyCommentary.com)

Kevin Orrick (McAlvanyWeeklyCommentary.com)

James Puplava (FinancialSense.com)

Chris Waltzek (Radio.Goldseek.com)*

George Norey (CoastToCoastAM.com)*

Doug Casey

Claudio Grass

Terry Coxon

Eric King

Jeff Thomas

*indirect contributors (radio and Internet broadcasts)

ABOUT THE AUTHORS

John Miller is a graduate of Georgetown University with a master's degree in public administration. John served as an artillery army spotter-pilot during the Vietnam era (serving in both Korea and the US). After military service, he began his career on Wall Street, working for many of Wall Street's top firms (Dean Witter, Interstate Securities, and Lehman Brothers). After 20 years in the securities business, he started his own investment firm, Miller & Associates. The firm began operations in Florida and subsequently relocated to Maui, Hawaii. John presently manages Miller & Associates, in Maui, Hawaii, and NZ Trans Global Investments, in Auckland, NZ.

John and his wife, Monica, moderate the Investment Club International. This Internet, *social* investment club is unique. It has over 600 members worldwide, is free, and is educational in nature. John writes for the Club Blog each week and does his best to answer questions from the membership.

He resides with Monica in Waiheke Island, New Zealand. The club's blog can be found on the website at *www.InvestmentClub International.ning.com.*

Monica Miller's career involved work as an international sales, marketing, and product development professional for the spa and beauty industry. Besides the US, she traveled frequently throughout Asia and Europe.

Monica was instrumental in forming and moderating the Maui Investment Club. She and John hosted the popular Maui radio talk show "The Investment Club." The show's format was similar to the popular "Doland's" radio show. It used old-time radio skits to teach the fundamentals of investing.

John and Monica Miller

Contents

Introduction 1

Chapter 1—The Coming Banking Holiday 5

Chapter 2—Getting Your CDs and Savings Accounts Overseas 11

Chapter 3—Safeguarding Your Stock Investments by Using an Overseas Custodian or by Direct Registration 21

Chapter 4—Uncle Sam Wants Your IRAs, 401Ks, 403B Plans, and Gold! 33

Chapter 5—Capital Controls 51

Chapter 6—A Look at a Suisse Precious Metals Depository 71

Chapter 7—"Reporting" 89

Chapter 8—Opening an Offshore Trust 97

Chapter 9—Getting Yourself Out of Dodge 103

Chapter 10—A Simple Plan to Keep Your Assets Safe from an Out-of-Control Government 117

Chapter 11—Porter Stansberry's Stern Message 133

Chapter 12—John Williams: The Coming Hyper-Inflation 173

Chapter 13—Don't Put all Your Eggs (Assets) in One Country 207

Chapter 14—The "Urgency" 213

Chapter 15—The Crash of 2012 219

Chapter 16—China's Secret Plan to Bankrupt Millions of Americans? 229

Summary 255

Conclusion 267

INTRODUCTION

WE DID IT!

As I sit down and write this book, with the help of my wife and partner, Monica, I can't help but being amazed at the beautiful scenery right outside my window. Waiheke Island is, by far, the most beautiful land that we have ever visited.

I am continuously amazed that we're actually here in New Zealand. While living in Hawaii, we had a NZ friend do a "Google Earth" search of Waiheke Island. He showed us Waiheke's beautiful beaches, which reminded us of Maui. Our house lease was expiring, and our investment club members knew we could take care of them just as well from NZ. So, with clear conscience, we called Air New Zealand, and we were on our way.

We really didn't intend to stay in NZ for any great length of time, as we love Maui. However, the longer we stayed, the more we did not want to leave. Our clients and investment club members needed to know how the NZ–Australian investment scene worked. They wanted to know how to get their investments and savings safely out of the US before capital controls set in. This required us to stay for at least three months.

Three months went by, and we got hooked. NZ is great, its people gracious and caring, and the scenery and countryside second to none. It is civilized, it has a great banking and investment system, and its people speak English! Adding it all up, we made our decision to stay. We rented a nice place, got our three-year visas, and began working toward residency.

We did return to Maui once to say our final goodbyes to all our friends and clients. That was in mid-2010.

THE COMING BANKING HOLIDAY

Gaining permanent residency in NZ is challenging. We were advised that there were a few ways to gain permanent residency. One is to work for a NZ company in your specialized field. This didn't apply to us, as we were over the age of 55. The other route that seemed to fit had to do with establishing your own business. This was called the "entrepreneurial work visa" program. We chose that route, and started NZ Trans Global Investments, Ltd. While establishing a financial advisory company in NZ is easy, getting one's financial license is not! After a year of intense study and examinations, I was awarded the highest accreditation, the title of "authorized financial adviser."

As an authorized financial adviser, I was permitted to join the prestigious "custodian firm" Aegis, Ltd. Custodian firms are unlike any financial firms in the US. Neither the firm, nor the adviser, has access to the client's investments, or funds; only the client does!

This is a far cry from US standards, which apparently enabled MF Global to have allegedly run off with $1.1 billion of client funds. Custodian firms in NZ safeguard the clients' assets; they could not possibly gain access to clients' funds even if they wanted to. Custodian firms here in NZ have no liabilities and are not permitted by law to risk their, or their clients', assets. Surprisingly, there are only two such firms: First NZ, Ltd. and Aegis, Ltd. As many of you know, many foreign banks and custodian companies do not welcome American accounts. Aegis did welcome American accounts as long as the adviser did his or her "due diligence." Thus, we chose Aegis for our account and recommended that our clients do the same.

Our clients were advised that they could easily open an account with Aegis. Once the account was opened, they could purchase CDs (term deposits), stocks, and mutual funds—actually, almost

INTRODUCTION

any investment on world markets. Money market accounts in NZ are called "overnight accounts," and they pay about 4%. Compare this with US money market accounts that pay virtually nothing.

Once we had access to Aegis, Ltd., and their superb financial platform, we started to bring over our Maui accounts. Our clients now love the NZ way of doing business. Not only is it safer, but custodian firms "pool" commissions for better (lower) rates.

The purpose of our book is to show our clients, club members, and readers exactly how we made the transition, and to prove to them that what we have now is better, and safer, than investing in the US. Americans can now diversify their investments safely and easily overseas, with our help.

Whether you use Aegis or not, you should join our "International Investment Club" (www.InvestmentClubInternational.ning.com). It's free and will keep you advised of any new reporting requirement. Not only that, but you will be able to meet and communicate with other investors worldwide.

The essays that I picked for the book are written by the best in their field, and the information is current. You will find that the chapters are timely and pertinent to our subject matter. Some of the experts that made the book possible include: Simon Black, Porter Stansberry, Gerald Celente, Dr. Steve Sjuggerud, John Williams, David McAlvany, Chris Waltzek, and James Puplava.

At the end of each chapter, Monica and I present our comments and advise how we handled, or are handling, each topic.

Onward.

CHAPTER ONE

The Coming Banking Holiday

"The Fed's behavior over the past 15 months has put America on a very dangerous path. The Fed has increased the monetary base (high-powered or wholesale money) by the largest amount ever, from colonial times to the present, times 10. Without an exit strategy, inflation is a virtual certainty over the coming decade, while an effective exit strategy virtually assures a further weakening of the US economy. Chairman Bernanke has put the US economy in a lose/lose situation."

—Arthur B. Laffer, economist

THE COMING BANKING HOLIDAY

It's happened before, it can happen again, and it can happen anywhere. In America, back in 1933, the government called a "bank holiday" to stop masses of depositors from pulling their money out of the banks. Now, in 2012, in America and around the world there are ominous economic times and the possibility of a repeat run on the banks cannot be dismissed.

As conditions deteriorate, particularly in the euro zone, our reiterated forecast for an economic 9/11 striking the equity markets is becoming increasingly plausible. In the event of a financial calamity, will a panicked public start pulling its money out of the markets and out of the banks? In such a scenario, how would governments respond? Would they, as they did back in 1933, make it illegal to own gold coins and gold bullion? Or now, with Big Brother knowing who bought what from whom, and when, would the government seize gold warehouse receipts, raid gold depositories, and, this time, even raid people's homes?

I WANT YOUR GOLD

Would the government force owners of gold to sell it to them at a deep discount price? Employing, verbatim, the language of the Gold Confiscation Act of 1933, Executive Order 6102, when President Franklin D. Roosevelt declared, "by the virtue of the authority vested in me by Section 5(b) of the Act of October 6, 1917..." etc., etc., he essentially decreed, "I'm going to take your gold from you and pay you what I want for it."

In 1933, the government made the people sell their gold to Uncle Sam at $20.57 an ounce. Immediately after the confiscation, the Federal Reserve jacked up the price to $35 an ounce, an increase of nearly 70 percent, thereby devaluing the dollar. It would take $35 in cash to buy what you used to be able to buy with a $20

1: THE COMING BANKING HOLIDAY

gold coin. If a bank holiday were called, would ATMs function, and if so, would they be limited to spitting out just a few dollars at a time? Would safety deposit boxes be seized? Would savings and checking accounts be frozen? Bank holiday? Confiscation? Won't happen! Can't happen again! Think Again!

Flashback to 2008, with the economy in tatters, Gerald Celente boldly warned of the strong possibility of a bank holiday being imposed following the inauguration of Barack Obama. He suggested that prudent *Trends Journal* subscribers "might consider preparing for such contingencies by having ready access to cash and gold. When banks reopen following a 'holiday,' limits may be set on withdrawal amounts and the currency may have been devalued, officially or de facto."

A bank holiday? Not a remote chance! The prospect was brushed off or ignored by the media. Celente's prediction was made at a time when the majority of the public, as well as the global financial markets, were on an emotional high believing the new President would deliver on campaign promises of "Hope" and "Change You Can Believe In." The best and brightest were on board with Obama, and plans were in place to regenerate the economy. The injection of billions of Fed stimulus dollars would generate millions of shovel-ready "Recovery" jobs and the good times would roll again. In reality, the economic pain and hardship that would hit people and businesses after the "Panic of '08" had just begun. As we wrote in 2008 and early 2009 when the first bailouts, rescue plans, Fed money injections, and stimulus plans were announced, they were just "cover-ups" and there would be no "Recovery." It was all smoke and mirrors, a confidence-building con job designed to make the public believe that recovery was at hand. As we would later learn, Washington's optimistic public face concealed its private awareness of the true nature of the financial damage left in the wake of the Panic.

In fact, the strong possibility of having to call a bank holiday was foremost on the minds of the new Administration. Was the White House reading the *Trends Journal*? Were they listening to Celente's forecast?

As Vice President Joe Biden admitted in June 2009, "Literally one of the early [discussions was] whether we might have to call a bank holiday...a bank holiday on the day after we were sworn in." "A bank holiday?" "A bank holiday on the day after we were sworn in?" Imagine! The entire economic system would come to a virtual standstill. "Holiday?" It would be no holiday and no picnic for the people unable to get their hands on their money. Moving Forward Now, in 2012, the public has lost confidence that world leaders, politicians and technocrats can solve the economic problems they had promised, but failed, to fix.

No longer heard are their encouraging words about sprouting "green shoots." Real world economic conditions have deteriorated far beyond what they were in 2009. Much of the real estate market has not recovered; those sectors and countries that escaped serious damage are now weakening, and countries whose housing markets soared are beginning to hear the bubbles bursting. Unemployment is as bad as ever, and in many places much worse. Unlike in 2009, when eurphoria was still in the air and the ECB chief could, with a straight face, express "confidence that the appropriate decisions will be taken" by the Greek government to resolve its problems, in 2011, those lines were laughable. And by 2012, Greece is but a minor problem within a pan-European sovereign debt crisis ...a crisis that was not even taken into consideration back in 2009 when the Obama White House was already contemplating a bank holiday. With trillions spent, lent and guaranteed by the EMU, ECB and IMF in an unsuccessful attempt to stem the debt crisis, the European financial fiasco has added a troubling dimension to global instability. The

1: THE COMING BANKING HOLIDAY

prospects for Economic Martial Law have gone commensurately global. Where to put your money, what currency to hold, and who to trust to hold it so that it would not be confiscated or frozen by the government were questions already being asked in 2011. Now, in 2012, the smart money around the world is taking proactive measures, or has plans in place to navigate their cash and themselves to safety in anticipation of a declaration of Economic Martial Law. Capital and wealthy citizens will be flying out of destabilized countries in search of safe havens for their money and/or themselves.

Trendpost: If financial factors alone are not enough to precipitate Economic Martial Law, emergency measures could be enacted in response to war or a terror strike (false flag or real). If so, will you be able to get your hands on your money in the event of a major attack? Do you remember what happened in the US on 9/11? Wall Street closed, and neither stocks nor CDs could be cashed out until it reopened a week later. Now, with the global economy so fragile and interdependent, a major strike anywhere would cause a financial panic everywhere. Governments could call a bank holiday. Or a cyber attack could sabotage the entire system, making withdrawals impossible.

Publisher's Note: The above bank holiday scenario is how I, as a trend analyst, see Economic Martial Law unfolding. (Gerald Celente)

Courtesy of Gerald Celente's Trends Journal, *Winter 2012*

THE COMING BANKING HOLIDAY

Our comment: Monica and I have been fans of Gerald Celente for the past 10 years. Our investment club members used to ask us at the end of each meeting: Do you think there will be a "banking holiday" next month? We always answered, "If you have 80% of your net worth in gold and silver, why should you care? Most US investors have zero in gold and silver, and when the banking holiday does occur, you will become rich, almost overnight, vis à vis those that had all their funds in cash at the bank."

Will there really be a banking holiday? It's our opinion that it's a 70/30% chance of it. Desperate nations do desperate things. Time permitting, the government will attempt to just "print its way out," inflating the national debt. However, if we do have a third world war or a major "event" (such as a 9/11), all bets are off; look for a banking holiday of sorts. The average American will wake up some morning and CNN will announce that all banks will be closed for a period of one week. At the end of this time, a new "red " currency will be available at a 50% conversion rate.

Our action: Starting in 2005, we put all 90% resources into gold and silver, and stored it in Switzerland. We maintained about 10% on hand to cover everyday expenses. We rent our home, we breakfast at the beach each day, we work each night from 2 a.m. to 10 a.m. helping our clients invest in gold and silver shares, and we live each day as it if were a coming banking holiday. Our 500 clients are well aware of this possibility, and we reinforce this with weekly newsletters.

CHAPTER TWO

Getting Your CDs and Savings Accounts Overseas

"Issue after issue of currency came; but no relief resulted. All men were waiting; stagnation became worse and worse. At last came the collapse and then a return, by a fearful shock, to a state of things which presented something like certainty of remuneration to capital and labor. There is a lesson in all this which it behooves every thinking man to ponder."

—Andrew White, *Fiat Money in France*

Instead of accepting the limiting banking choices offered by your hometown bank, you can open a foreign bank account in US dollars, or alternative currencies, or store gold in a private vault overseas. We'll discuss buying and storing gold in a subsequent chapter. This diversifies and protects your assets, taking your nest egg out of a single sovereign basket subject to the increasing rules and regulations of the US

It is 100% legal for a US citizen to open an offshore bank account—at least for now. Desperate governments don't hesitate to enact capital controls, designed to prevent the free flow of capital from crossing borders and good ol' Uncle Sam is already at work trying to prevent US citizens from protecting their assets in offshore accounts.

I want to make a point here. What I'm referring to here is protecting your assets by moving them out of America's political reach. Keep in mind, I am not advising, in any way, hiding your assets to avoid taxes. In any event, with capital controls just around the corner, it is the time now to take action to protect your assets while you still can. **When capital controls are imposed,** *you can always bring your savings and assets back to the US, should you wish, but you can't do it the other way around. Better safe than sorry!*

Having an offshore bank account is a fundamental part of international diversification. It's especially important in times like these when currency controls and government regulations are getting stricter, supposedly, "to battle money laundering and international terrorism." Offshore banking gives you a way of having part of your wealth outside of your country, so that you never risk having one government freeze or confiscate all your assets. Governments, especially the US Government, can freeze and confiscate your assets without even having to prove

2: GETTING YOUR CDS AND SAVINGS ACCOUNTS OVERSEAS

their case. They might just act on a hunch. How would you feel like waking up one day with your credit cards not working and finding out all your accounts are frozen indefinitely? It can take months, or even years, of lengthy court hearings before you get your money back. How are you going to afford a lawyer if your bank accounts are frozen?

A foreign bank account is an important diversification "flag" to plant abroad. You really want to consider jurisdictions with low taxes, a strong and stable financial sector, and one without a history of plundering the banks in bad times. A point worth mentioning is that offshore banking is not about hiding your money from the taxman, it is about diversifying your sovereign risks.

Often times, you'll also find that offshore interest rates are far better than domestic ones—if this comes as a surprise for you, it is not your fault. For obvious reasons, domestic banks are not going to tell you that you can get a much better return just by having your money in a foreign bank account. Not to mention the fact that foreign banks are likely to be stronger than banks in your home country.

Places where you will find the best offshore bank include countries like Switzerland, Hong Kong, Singapore, UAE, Qatar, and a few others (such as Australia & NZ, author added). An "Offshore" bank doesn't necessarily have to be located in a so-called "tax haven". Several of the countries mentioned above are spared of the tax haven-stamp that many other low tax countries have. Some banks require you to deposit and maintain a balance of at least $5000 in your account, but there are also banks where you can open an account and deposit as little as a few hundred dollars.

More About Opening An Offshore Bank Account

There is a bevy of information and misinformation out there about offshore banking. Some say it's illegal (it certainly isn't), while some say it's a great way to hide money and not worry about paying taxes (you'll end up in jail). As always, do your due diligence before you make any major decisions regarding your finances, and preferably get advice from a professional.

Offshore Bank Account: How to Get One and Why

Access to NZ and Australian banking, for Americans, is still possible if US persons are willing to jump through a few extra hoops. It entails using a financial intermediary known as an Independent Financial Management Company (IFMC) or Independent Asset Manager (IAM). The procedure is straightforward: The US client would establish an account with an IFMC/IAM, who would then open a banking relation in the name of the client.

For example, many of our conservative, CD-type clients are disappointed with the miserly ½% yields offered by weak US banks. By using our recommended Aegis, Ltd. financial management company in NZ, they are able to easily open an account and purchase a one-month Australian CD that is presently paying about 4¼% interest. Now here's a possible bonus: The US dollar, due to over-printing, is heading down, while the Australian dollar, with all its resources, is heading up. No guarantees here, but it is likely that the Australian dollar could rise another 10% against the US greenback. If this occurs, the 10% added to the 4¼% current yield would give you a potential 14%+ overall yield. As the US dollar continues to fall, expect the Australian dollar to rise farther. A word of caution: While highly unlikely, the scenario could go the other way, with the US dollar rising and the Aussi dollar falling, but the trend is definitely "up" for the Australian dollar.

2: GETTING YOUR CDS AND SAVINGS ACCOUNTS OVERSEAS

As you would expect, there are advantages and drawbacks to using this structure.

One big plus is that the client, through the IFMC/IAM, would have access to a wide range of financial and investment products not available from a bank, as well as professional investment advice tailored to the clients' goals and risk tolerance.

Another positive is the fact that most IFMCs and IAMs have low investment minimums, typically in the US$25,000 range. Trading, account, and administration fees in NZ and Australia are relatively low, due to a "pooling arrangement." For example, if an investor wishes to purchase a one-month term deposit (CDs, as they are called in America), his order may be pooled with $5,000,000 of other investors' money. By doing this, the small investor gets a better (higher) interest rate than he would have going solo.

One cannot forget "the safety factor!" NZ banks, with the exception of Kiwi Bank, which is 100% owned by the NZ government, are essentially divisions of the strong Australian banking sector. Australian banks are considered some of the strongest and safest banks in the world. Historically, when an economic event has taken place, the Australian government is quick to "jump in and protect" Australian bank depositors. Australia itself has little or no debt, and the country is awash with abundant natural resources.

Yesterday's traditional road to a NZ/Australian bank account has changed, and will likely face further course corrections as planned US reporting requirements are introduced or implemented in the years ahead. For those delaying moving assets to NZ/Australia, it may be unwise. With the uncertain future of access to international financial options, action must be taken sooner rather than later.

Before we leave the topic, let's address the question: "Can the US government still freeze your bank accounts even though they are offshore?" As it stands today, the answer is "no". While conditions may change in the future, it behooves us to get an account established now, before probable "capital controls" are put in place. If you wait until then, you'll definitely be out of luck.

Courtesy of Simon Black, Sovereign Man

A Good Safe Place for Your Savings

In short, the US government is in hock to its eyeballs... And Europe is in worse shape than the US But according to the IMF, Australia will be net debt free by 2020.

While the US government will stay busy printing money, the Australian government will stay busy cashing mining royalty checks with no end in sight.

You see, the Australian government owns the mineral and petroleum resources of Australia. (That's different from the US, where mineral rights can be privately owned.) And that makes Australia rich...Australia is chock-full of commodities that are in demand all around the globe.

I remember standing in Iceland a couple years ago, staring at a massive aluminum smelter that was a few city blocks long. The raw bauxite was shipped in from Australia—as far across the planet as you could get. In short, the far corners of the world need bauxite...and Australia has it.

Aluminum is only a tiny part of the big story of Australia's commodity reserves... Australia leads the world in "economically recoverable reserves" in many commodities...lead, zinc, uranium, nickel, and more. It ranks second in the world in economically recoverable reserves in gold, silver, copper, and more, according to the Australian Bureau of Statistics.

And then there's "China's Gold"—iron ore... the raw material in steel making. China needs it...Australia's got it.

"Where on earth is your money safe these days?" That is THE question. When you look at the debt trends, it's NOT safe in America. And it's NOT safe in Europe.

But the fact that the Australian government owns its resources, and it will be net debt free by 2020, makes Australia a safe country for your money. In a way, the nation's currency—the Australian dollar issued by the government—is solidly "backed" by the country's vast natural resources, owned by the government.

And the Australian dollar is paying you to own it. Right now, you earn next-to-nothing in interest on your money in the bank in US dollars and euros. But in Australia, astoundingly, you earn 4.25% interest on your cash.

The major risk here is what happens to Australia if China crashes? There's no mistaking the fact that the Australian dollar is highly correlated to commodity prices. Exports of iron and coal alone make up 39% of Australia's total merchandise exports. If China stops buying, Australia will take a big hit.

However, I think the Australian government is in better shape to handle a crisis than any country in the world. The typical government "tools" to fight back a crisis are to 1) borrow money and 2) cut interest rates. With no debt and a very high (4.25%) deposit rate, Australia has plenty of room to do both today.

I could go on. But you get the idea.

For the long run, Australia's dollar is safe. And with high interest rates, it's good for the short-run, too. Australia might just be the last safe country on earth for your money. So consider Australia...

Courtesy of Dr. Steve Sjuggerud, True Wealth

2: GETTING YOUR CDS AND SAVINGS ACCOUNTS OVERSEAS

Our comment: As soon as we arrived in NZ, we transferred our savings accounts from the Bank of Hawaii to ASB Bank of New Zealand. Our interest rate overnight rose from .5% to 4%. The NZ dollar, when we arrived in 2009, was $.50 against the US dollar. Needing a car, we headed off to Auckland Center and found an almost-new 2001 BMW with low mileage. The sticker price was $10,000, and we were all set to write a check out for that amount. The salesman said: "That'll be $5,000 in US dollars."

Our action: As soon as I became a licensed authorized investment adviser in NZ, we moved our ASB account over to Aegis, Ltd., our new custodian. At Aegis, we could purchase a one-month pooled CD (called a term deposit here). Our interest rate rose to 4.67% from 4%, and we only had to tie our funds up for a few more days (not months). Finding Aegis, an American-friendly custodian, was a godsend. Monica and I immediately began advising our clients of this new discovery, and began transferring investment accounts from America to New Zealand.

CHAPTER THREE

Safeguarding Your Stock Investments by Using an Overseas Custodian or by Direct Registration

"Nothing will unnerve the paper gold shorts more quickly and do more to undercut their confidence than to strip them of the real metal and force them to come up with more hard gold bullion to make good on deliveries. "Stand and Deliver or Go Home" should be the rallying cry of the gold longs to the paper gold shorts."

—Trader Dan Norcini

THE COMING BANKING HOLIDAY

*I*n this chapter, we're going to explore the ways of safeguarding our securities. In NZ, the securities industry makes use of custodian investment firms. They cannot fail, as they have no liabilities; they'll be discussed later in the chapter, and are highly recommended. If you can't or won't bring your investments to NZ, then by all means get your shares "directly registered" in the US. The brokerage industry has changed a great deal since I first started with Hayden Stone, Inc. back in 1967, so be careful!

What good is picking the right stock, only to see its loss during a brokerage firm's liquidation? In the author's opinion, there are two ways to safeguard your shares, really safeguard them:

The first involves making use of a custodian if you have your shares overseas. We'll discuss this second option first.

The second involves using "direct registration" if holding your shares in the US. We'll discuss this in the latter part of the chapter.

Using a Custodian to Hold Your Shares When Your Account Is Overseas

A custodian is not a bank, it is a separate entity, without *any* liabilities, nor can they assume liabilities, or take risks of any kind. They were designed to protect and safeguard clients' investments *after* they are purchased from a securities broker. Or, as many Americans are now doing, transferring their investments *from* their American brokerage firms, to an overseas "custodian."

The custodian, through a "separate account," holds investments on your behalf. This is an efficient way of administering investments as it enables "the custodian" to aggregate (i.e., combine) the purchase or sale of an investment on behalf of a large number of investors, and transact this in the market as a single instruction. It also enables the custodian, to receive consolidated interest and dividend payments, which it then allocates to individual investors' portfolios.

In other words, aggregation enables the custodian, the ability to undertake less investment transactions with fund providers and security brokers. This aggregation ability is one of the reasons why fees for managed funds purchased through the custodian, are often cheaper than if purchased directly. Through aggregation, the custodian can often avoid investors being charged minimum brokerage fees for listed investments that might otherwise be charged for small transactions.

The custodian acts as a bare trustee and has no discretionary powers, so it cannot undertake investment transactions without instructions from you, or your authorized representatives. Although the custodian's "separate account" is the registered holder of investments, *you* retain the beneficial ownership of your investments.

Compare this with brokers in the US that hold their clients' securities in "street name." By holding securities in this manner, US brokerage firms can, in essence, gamble with their clients' funds, much the same way as MF Global did. While the US may advertise the fact that they, too, offer custodian services for their clients' funds, US custodians are part of large banks. With the US banking system in peril, you want to stay as far away from the large banks as possible. If the US bank goes under, so could the US custodian. This cannot happen with overseas custodians.

How Does the Custodian Insure the Client's Money (Investments) is Safe?

An important function of the custodian service is the safekeeping of your investments. Investment professionals using the custodial service are not required to handle your money.

To add cash into your portfolio, you simply deposit the amount directly into the custodian's "separate account" (trust account). The custodian then insures the cash is added to your portfolio. Any cash withdrawals you require from your portfolio are paid directly into your nominated bank account. The cash cannot be sent to a third party, as in the US. As a further safeguard, the custodian must examine (have in their possession), an original (not copy) of the client's bank deposit slip. This extra step completely eliminates any possibility of the adviser, or a third party, gaining access to the clients' funds.

You can transfer existing investments into your custodian portfolio by transferring their ownership to the custodian's "separate account." This enables the custodian to administer these investments for you, while you retain beneficial ownership of your investments.

Interest and dividend payments from your investments are automatically added to your custodian cash account and retained in your portfolio. Purchases of investments and proceeds from your investment sales are deducted or added to your custodian cash account.

By having your investments held via a custodian, you do not have to worry about the significant, ongoing paperwork and administration that is associated with investing.

It is important to note that none of your investment professionals, the custodian, or the "separate account" guarantees the performance of the investments in your portfolio. Investments are subject to investment risk including loss of income and capital invested."

Courtesy of Monica Miller

Establishing "Direct Registration" for Your Shares

Please do not sleep on my dear friends. If you do nothing, you may very well have nothing in the end.

If you do not want to get it in the end you will have to act now on what I have already told you. The material contained in here concerning the system and market events is correct, even though it proposes its own solution. I should know. I have owned brokerage and clearing houses.

The answer lies, in my opinion, in going to direct registration at the transfer agent and out of the clearing agent and ultimately, where possible, to paper certificates. If the company you are invested in does not participate in direct registration and also does not issue paper certificates, raise hell with them.

Do you own gold and silver mining stocks? Or any stocks for that matter? Even if you say, "yes," chances are you don›t really own them. It is one of the dirtiest little secrets in the brokerage business. And 99.9% of people have no idea it is even being done to them. It's called "street name registration" and it's how the brokerage where you hold your stocks "registers" your shares. To save money and time, and to allow your shares to be included as assets that they can use to do what they want with, your brokerage never actually registers you as an owner of the shares.

Street name registration allows your broker to lend your shares to short sellers, thereby driving down the price of your own stocks. Additionally, this method allows your broker to "re-hypothecate" your assets—meaning it allows your broker to borrow money against your shares and speculate in the derivatives market.

These hidden risks are planting the seeds of tomorrow's ultimate collapse—In which there may be a system-wide collapse of broker dealers, taking down millions of investors, and ensuring permanent non-recoverable losses to an entire generation!

MF Global Was Just the First to Go Down

MF Global investors found out first hand just how secure their funds were. Most don't realize it, but MF Global was a clearinghouse for both stocks and futures. Like many/most brokerages, they "invest" their own funds, often on a highly leveraged basis, to earn income. But, with the recent collapse of Greek government bonds and with MF Global's highly leveraged position in them, MF Global was bankrupted in an instant.

The problem is, they tried to cover their losses with their customer's own funds. You see, unless your shares are registered in your own name—a process that isn't that difficult or costly—your brokerage considers it as assets they can use for their own needs. Plus, once a brokerage goes bankrupt (which is something we expect to happen very often over the coming years) if you hadn't personally registered your shares then your shares go down as assets of the brokerage and are used to pay off their creditors.

3: SAFEGUARDING YOUR STOCK INVESTMENTS...

"Several million private accounts may vanish—brokerage accounts, pension funds, mutual funds, they're all at risk. We are getting into the middle stages of implosion, where I believe the public will not wake up until at least one million private accounts are stolen, and completely vanish."

—Jim Willie, *The Hat Trick Letter*

The Western Financial System Is in a State of Collapse

The reason for this coming broker-dealer crisis is simple. The entire western financial system is built on debt—it's an anti-capitalist system set-up to make the rich richer and the poor poorer. It started in 1913 with the founding of the Federal Reserve, it went further down the slippery slope with gold confiscation in the US in 1933 and reached the beginning of the end in 1971 with Nixon closing the gold window, turning the US dollar (officially called the Federal Reserve Note) into a completely fiat currency.

In more recent times, it was the repeal of the Glass-Steagel Act that allowed investment banks to acquire broker-dealers, and pass the risks of 100-1 leverage downstream to all client accounts. Therefore, your stock investments are now only as safe as the speculative portfolio of your broker-dealer. Considering most Western Investment Houses are leveraged at least 40-1, this means your stocks are no safer than a 40-1 bet on European bonds (with which most western investment banks are leveraged to the teeth).

Some believe their stocks will be protected by the Securities Investor Protection Corporation (SIPC), which insures stocks accounts from broker collapse up to $500k for securities, and account cash balances up to $250k. But what if you have more than $250k in cash and/or more than $500k of securities in your account? What if one of the largest broker dealers in the country went bust, bringing down thousands of accounts and depleting the entire reserves of the SIPC? What if the SIPC itself goes bankrupt? What few people are aware of, is that the SIPC only carries about $1 billion in funds to cover investors! This means only one or two high profile broker dealer bankruptcies will be enough to completely wipe out the SIPC.

Some may claim the US government will bail out the SIPC to whatever extent needed. But what if two major broker dealers went bust while at the same time the US government suffers a major Treasury bond auction failure? This is all but a certainty in the coming years.

And the same thing applies in Canada to Canadian brokerages and Canadian stocks. The Canadian economy is intricately tied to the US. In fact, not many people are aware, but all that backs the Canadian dollar is the US dollar. The Canadian Government sold all its gold decades ago. The entire monetary & financial system is headed for its final destination—total collapse…and 2008 was just the beginning.

"If you were lucky enough not to be a customer of MF Global ... then you should view the MFG episode as a warning shot. You might not get another warning shot."

—Steven Saville, *The Speculative Investor*

One Last Bubble?

But, we've been predicting there are still a few more years left… not 10. But maybe two to three more years…or a little more. We believe the Federal Reserve and all western central banks will

3: SAFEGUARDING YOUR STOCK INVESTMENTS...

print enough money to get the system through for another few years...just enough for them to get out of office and retired to their Caribbean island villas before all the western fiat currencies enter hyperinflation.

And, we believe this will create one final bubble. The tech bubble is dead. The housing bubble is dead. And the bubble in government debt is in its death throes. What will be the final bubble? It will be in gold and silver mining stocks. But the question remains—how can we safely invest in gold and silver mining shares and avoid the collapse brought on by the coming broker dealer crisis?

There are two methods of owning stocks your broker-dealer will never tell you about. These two methods completely remove the broker dealer counter party risk attached to your shares—effectively removing them from "the system."

These two methods deprive your broker dealer the abilities to sell your stocks short and to "re-hypothecate" them. Your broker dealer will never willingly tell you about these methods—because they make more money when your shares are in their hands—precisely where risks are greatest to you.

These methods are so safe, that even if your broker dealer collapsed tomorrow, and stole every penny from every client investment account you would be able to sleep safe and sound, knowing your stocks are far out of reach, and legally unavailable to access by your broker-dealer.

This means everyone—all brokers in the Unites States and Canada. If every broker collapsed tomorrow due to waves of bankruptcies, these ownership methods will protect you 100%. You will be able to sleep safe and sound at night, knowing your shares are carrying zero counter party risk.

That's why we've supported Tekoa Da Silva, a bright young man and publisher of *BullMarketThinking.com* in putting together a complete research paper outlining the process to register your shares and giving you all the info you need to know to do it easily, quickly and properly. He spent hundreds of hours dealing with broker dealers, transfer agents, public companies, and the SIPC in researching and finding out all the details on how to get your shares outside of the system. We've put all his research together into a Special Report called "Bulletproof Shares." You can get more information and purchase this report at tdv.bulletproofshares.com.

The Greatest Buying Opportunity of a Generation

There will be more opportunity in this crisis than in any other in the past century. But, in order to profit from the coming crisis you need to ensure that if/when your brokerage goes bankrupt you still retain ownership of your shares. Shares are proof of ownership of a real asset and don't depend on a stock exchange or a brokerage...as long as you make sure you register them properly.

If you are able to preserve and accumulate wealth during the collapse, you will be offered the greatest buying opportunity of our generation. Blue-chip companies may be purchased for pennies on the dollar...but the trick is to safely protect your assets until we reach that point.

We've been covering the ongoing collapse of the western financial system and we've been adamant that there are two main ways to protect yourself, and profit from the collapse by owning gold and silver bullion and the miners who produce precious metals.

3: SAFEGUARDING YOUR STOCK INVESTMENTS...

Owning gold and silver bullion will protect your assets...and owning shares in the miners will likely result in massive profits. However, this multi-generational profit opportunity will only present itself for those who can make it through the collapse with ownership of their shares intact. Unless you've gone through the process outlined in *Bulletproof Shares* then you don't really own your stocks...your broker does.

Please protect yourself now and pass this along to anyone you know who owns US or Canadian traded stocks before it is too late.

Courtesy of Jeff Berwick

Our comment: As a broker starting in the business in 1967, with John Templeton, Bob Chapman, and Don McAlvany (and numerous others), I never gave a second thought as to the security of my clients' investments. They were always safe; why would they not be? Then SIPC came about, reinforcing the theme. It was not until the MF Global episode that I realized how fragile US security was. How could MF Global gamble with clients' sacred funds and lose, and the governing body (the COMEX) not make good for the loss suffered by investors? Gerald Celente, and thousands more, lost hundreds of thousands of dollars in the "letdown." I was about halfway though this book when the MF Global incident occurred; it forever changed the way I have guided and will guide in the future my clients' future investments.

Our action: Bringing over our investment account from Scottrade, which I loved, to Aegis, was a no-brainer (and this was before the MF Global mess). The safety issue was paramount. I just didn't feel my brokerage account was safe in the US. Bringing it over to NZ, and depositing the securities into a custodial account, seemed to be the prudent thing to do. The cost was about the same, and the ability to buy foreign stocks was almost limitless, as I could buy almost any stock, on any exchange worldwide, without any difficulty. The commissions were extraordinarily low, as they were pooled. I was delighted with what I saw, and I began to advise clients of my new discovery. To date, about 30% of our accounts have come over. With the release of this book, I expect to have my hands full opening new accounts. I look forward to it. Oh, by the way, the advisory fees here are half of what they are in the US. The results are better, and the safety factor is priceless.

CHAPTER FOUR

Uncle Sam Wants Your IRAs, 401Ks, 403B Plans, and Gold!

"Freedom is never more than one generation away from extinction. We didn't pass it to our children in the bloodstream. It must be fought for, protected, and handed on for them to do the same."

—Ronald Reagan

THE COMING BANKING HOLIDAY

Uncle Sam Has Plans for Your IRA, 401K, 403B, and Gold

In the near future, the US government may be planning to take over your 401K and Individual Retirement Accounts (IRAs) and managing them on its own.

It's bad and getting worse. Uncle Sam is broke and desperate. He's got his eyes on your money (including your 401Ks, IRAs, and other retirement accounts), and unless you take action NOW to get it out of his reach, he'll grab it faster than your plan administrator can take their fees.

It's already happened in several countries around the world including Ireland, Argentina, Bulgaria, Hungary, and Poland. And US politicians are already talking about doing it, too, so this is a real threat. Think about it: The same group of people whose fiscal irresponsibility got us into this mess wants to take charge of managing your retirement accounts. It sounds like a recipe for disaster.

And there's more BAD NEWS. Many are widely predicting…

The Death of Fiat Currencies

Declining Value of the US Dollar (USD)

4: UNCLE SAM WANTS YOUR IRAS, 401KS, 403B PLANS, AND GOLD!

Contrary to popular (and very misguided) belief, the US Dollar is NOT a "safe haven." It's more like a sinking ship. In fact, since 1913 the US Dollar has lost 95% of its value in relation to gold. Yet the vast majority of Americans have no idea how rapidly the purchasing power of their dollars is declining.

Inflation is also eroding the purchasing power of US Dollars. The "official" inflation rate reported by the US government may be low…but that's mostly because they constantly change the calculation to keep it artificially low. If inflation was measured today the way it was measured in the 1970's, the inflation rate would be approaching 10%.

If you currently hold assets in these dying currencies, the time to act is NOW!

The buying power of your dollars declines by nearly 10% each year. If you're not making at least 10% on your money, then you are actually LOSING money measured in terms of purchasing power.

And if you think this applies only to the US Dollar, you're dead wrong! Many experts argue the death of fiat currencies is near. The Euro, the Yen, and the Pound aren't faring much better than the US Dollar as stores of value. They are all headed towards the intrinsic value of the paper they are printed on…which is ZERO!!

Here's the BOTTOM LINE:

Holding all your assets in the US Dollar (or any single fiat currency) is financial suicide. Unless you take measures to protect yourself your dollar-denominated assets are going to collapse in value and your standard of living will be painfully lower.

"It is imprudent to hold everything in one currency."

—Alan Greenspan, former Federal Reserve Chairman

Let's recap the major Sovereign Risks to your Assets:

- The Impending System Reset (the old system of debt and consumption has gone up in flames and the new rules have yet to be written)

- Unsustainable Fiscal Irresponsibility (for decades governments have run huge deficits and taken on massive amounts of debt to cover them and this is NOT sustainable)

- Lawsuits (particularly in the US, it's easy to lose everything in a lawsuit—and frivolous lawsuits are commonplace)

- Immediate or Retroactive Taxes and Fees (broke governments will not hesitate to quickly pass legislation aimed at transferring your wealth to their greedy little hands)

- Asset Seizures (any judge, bureaucrat, or police agency can freeze or seize your assets in the blink of an eye—and you're guilty until proven innocent)

- Capital Controls (desperate governments routinely enact laws aimed at controlling your assets and restricting the free flow of capital across borders)

- Currency Debasement & Inflation (inflationary policies and constant increases in the supply of money decrease the purchasing power of your money)

- Government Takeover of Retirement Accounts (don't be surprised when Uncle Sam passes legislation to take over and manage the funds in your 401(k) and IRA accounts someday soon)

- And there are more—too many to mention here—but you get the idea.

4: UNCLE SAM WANTS YOUR IRAS, 401KS, 403B PLANS, AND GOLD!

So How Do You Diversify Sovereign Risk?

If this sounds like a hopeless situation, don't worry because it's entirely possible to manage all these risks. In fact, thousands of smart people just like you are already doing it. It goes back to the NEW Global Principal of Diversification and what I call planting multiple flags.

Simply put, if you don't have all your assets under the control of a single government you have diversified your sovereign risk because no single government has control over your assets. It's a simple concept and it's perfectly legal.

Think about how things work under the old system—people are effectively given pre-packaged options for the major decisions in their lives. There are pre-defined career paths for becoming a doctor, a lawyer, a pilot, a nurse, and almost any other profession you can imagine.

When it comes to retirement planning, you just answer a menu of questions to define your risk profile and instantly you have a model portfolio to follow. There's little thinking involved… and little choice either considering the limited number of mutual funds available in most retirement accounts.

How the US Government Will Seize Your Retirement Account

Following in the footsteps of a rather ignominious list of nations like Argentina and Hungary, the government of Ireland is set to take its 'fair share' of private retirement funds.

Drowning in debt and faced with unpopular, unrealistic, ridiculously unpopular austerity measures, the government has announced that it will now tax private pension savings in order to raise 470 million Euros (roughly $675 million) per year…a lot of money in a country of only 4.4 million people.

Somehow, the government expects to be able to create 100,000 jobs to bring down an unemployment rate at 14.7%. Perhaps they plan on hiring 100,000 new workers to go around the country and collect the tax.

It reminds me of what I saw in Bolivia a couple of weeks ago– there's a tax or toll or fee for nearly everything you do. Driving on the highway (if you can call it that) outside of Santa Cruz, you pay a toll…obviously not for the maintenance of the road, but to pay the salary of the toll collector.

At the airport, you have to pay an airport tax before departure… obviously not for the upkeep and efficiency of the airport (it took 2-hours to make it to my gate), but to pay the salaries of the guys who collect the airport tax.

This is what politicians consider 'job creation,' yet these positions only serve to destroy value. That they would stick up the retirement funds of hard working people is even more immoral.

Here's the best part, though. If you are a government worker in Ireland, your pension is exempt. They're only going after people in the private work force. It's truly disgusting logic to force private workers to pay for years of political incompetence while absolving government employees.

Coincidentally, there are a few other loopholes as well, particularly for non-residents and non-resident funds. Apparently those Irish who saw the writing on the wall and got busy moving themselves and their assets offshore will get to keep all of their savings.

Ireland is not the first country to call this play, nor will it be the last. Pension funds are attractive targets for politicians who have

4: UNCLE SAM WANTS YOUR IRAS, 401KS, 403B PLANS, AND GOLD!

wide eyes and the most carnal thoughts at the site of any large pool of cash.

Think it can't happen where you live? Think again. Late last year, the *French government* went through an elaborate process to change its pension laws, "legally" allowing politicians to steal retirement funds from the public in order to pay off other debts.

In the US, public pensions have been raided for years, Congress routinely 'borrows' from Social Security to make up budget shortfalls. This is what talking heads mean when they play down concerns of a $14 trillion debt "because we owe it to ourselves" $4.6 trillion of the debt is owed to intergovernmental agencies like Social Security.

Chances of this money being repaid to Social Security in full? Slim. The trend is more debt, not paying off existing debt. In fact, I'm convinced that politicians have their eyes firmly fixed on the trillions of dollars in private, individual retirement accounts (IRAs) in the United States to fund new spending.

Here's how it will go down:

First, there will be some event…some sort of financial cataclysm, similar to the market meltdown we saw in 2008 after Lehman.

Bear in mind that most IRAs are managed by boneheads at big financial institutions; they get compensated not based on the performance of their portfolio, but on the total amount of assets under management. Your interests and their interests do not align.

As such, most IRAs are callously tossed into S&P index funds or some such generic vehicle, citing the safety of broader market diversification, as if that nonsense they teach in MBA finance classes is how the real world actually works.

THE COMING BANKING HOLIDAY

When a big crash occurs, these unhedged broad market positions get hammered the most. Don't worry though, your fund manager will still get a big fat bonus check, because his performance is irrelevant.

This is when Congress will step in. Citing its desire to "protect" the American people from future market shocks, the politicians will mandate that a portion of all managed retirement funds be invested in the "safety and security" of US Treasury bonds. And, just to be on the safe side, let's park them in 30-year bonds that yield 4.35%.

Sound fair? Well who asked you anyways…just be a good citizen and turn over your money already. The important part is that the big financial institutions still get their big fat fees, and the government gets its hands on the mother lode.

This is how US taxpayers will end up being forced to loan their hard earned retirement savings to the government at rates far below any expected inflation.

Right now, there is a window of opportunity to take action; US taxpayers with retirement accounts can set up a special kind of IRA structure that allows you to take control of your retirement savings, and even ship it offshore if you want to, completely legitimately.

After taking control of your IRA, you can do any number of things—buy and store gold and silver coins overseas; hold foreign currencies in an *offshore bank account*; buy securities on international stock exchanges; purchase agricultural property overseas, or even a beautiful apartment on the beach in some sunny country.

The possibilities are incredible…but the most important thing is that you get this retirement money off the radar of the politicians before they pull an Ireland and announce some new measure, virtually overnight. These things can happen very, very quickly.

I've talked about this before a number of times, and every time I read the news of yet another country taking this approach, it serves as a reminder to take action.

Courtesy of Simon Black, Sovereign Man

The Government Wants to Steal Your 401k

4.3 Trillion dollars sits in our nation's 401k Retirement Plans. It's too big a temptation for the Federal government to ignore, and we may be on the verge of a full-scale attack against our citizens' privately held wealth.

I'll get to the details of that in a moment. For the benefit of our foreign readers, a 401k is a retirement plan. The advantage of a 401k is that all money put into it can be taken as a tax deduction against your income. So, in effect, the government subsidizes a good portion of your retirement savings. This is one of the greatest gifts the Federal government has ever given us, because our money is allowed to compound completely tax-free!

Now it's not all gravy—you can't touch this money until you are 59 1/2, and when you start pulling money out you are taxed at ordinary income levels. This is regardless of whether your gains came from long-term capital gains or dividend income. At this time, ordinary income rates are, generally speaking (depending upon your tax bracket), higher than capital gains rates and dividend income rates.

So the government gets their money in the end, which is why these are considered tax deferred plans, not tax-free plans.

The advantage for the saver to contributing to a 401k is that contributions are tax deductible, meaning they get to grow their money for decades without the relentless performance drag of having to pay capital gains and dividend income tax each year.

This means that the government is providing you with an ongoing interest free loan for the life of your 401k. This "loan" allows you to compound more money...faster...for free. You are using other peoples' money (OPM)—in this case the government's money—to boost your gains.

For years this has been a phenomenal wealth creation tool for everyday Americans, *but this great gift could be under serious threat.*

The Unions Want Your Money

The unions have a problem: They have massive pension obligations that are woefully under funded. Some reports indicate that their pension funds are only 62% funded, with total shortfalls approaching $165 billion.

Their approach is to convince the government to take custody of ALL 401k assets and effectively nationalize them into a government guaranteed annuity that will pay about 3%. That's a rate that will guarantee that you lose money after inflation.

One of the largest contributors to the Obama cause is the Services Employees International Union (SEIU). They are the "face" organization behind this plan to centralize America's savings into "Guaranteed Retirement Accounts" (GRA's).

Now, guess where those 4 trillion 401k dollars will end up being invested?

4: UNCLE SAM WANTS YOUR IRAS, 401KS, 403B PLANS, AND GOLD!

The recipient of all this largesse will be US treasuries. This is a triple win for the Obama administration, the Federal government, and the unions:

The unions get to bail out their under funded pension funds by delivering guaranteed returns which, as measly as they are, are better than zero returns. The democrats get to return the favor back to the unions for their long-term support. And the Federal government gets to use our money to help fund the federal deficit.

The sales pitch being used is that this should be done to save Americans from the "emotional ups and downs" of the stock market! How galling is that?

But even if this nationalization effort fails to pass, savers are still being assaulted by the Obama administration.

Let me explain.

In the most recent budget, the President is proposing restricting the amount of money investors can put into 401k's! The President's administration apparently feels that the best way forward is to PUNISH SAVERS!

Not only that, but we also saw that the President wants to boost dividend taxes from the current 15% to a whopping 40%! The actual top bracket with the inclusion of the Obama Care tax will be 43.5%. Oh, but don't worry, because this is just for those evil bloodsuckers making $250k a year.

Let me tell you something, depending upon where you live, $250k is not a lot of money. Even if you live in a low cost area of the country, $250k does not make you one of the glittering rich.

You might not be rich right now, but it is every American's right to strive to become rich if they so desire. That's a big part of the

American dream—work hard, build a business, live beneath your means and enjoy the fruits of your labor. It is precisely that striving for personal greatness that makes our entire country great.

Why should the entire nation be held to the standards of people who can't make good decisions for themselves? It is not only wrong, but it is destructive to our way of life. We are a people that firmly believe in the right to determine the direction of our own lives. We don't need a bunch of narrow-minded Washington pukes telling us what's good for us.

It is not unimaginable that this legislation will pass, because crazier things have happened in our country's history. For instance, back in 1933 under Executive Order 6102, all privately held gold was confiscated by the US government.

You were compelled to sell your gold to the Federal Reserve for $20 an ounce under penalty of 10 years in prison. The Federal Reserve then promptly sold the bulk of the gold for $35 an ounce to the Europeans while pocketing the difference.

What's to say that they won't do the same thing with our 401ks?

Courtesy of Teeka Tiwari, creator, ETF Master Trader and the Tycoon Report

Terry Coxon Wrote the Book: Unleash Your IRA; Passport IRA Tells You How to Implement It

The staff at Passport IRA is dedicated to one mission– providing its clients with the timeliest, most cost effective, professional assistance in the business to establish an Open Opportunity IRA.

Our team understands all the details and all the steps for putting an Open Opportunity IRA together, and has helped helped thousands of investors understand and set up these structures. We'll answer all of your questions, give you a reality check on your plan (and perhaps show you some good ways to improve it), and most importantly, put all the pieces together for you so that you can focus on generating much higher, tax-free returns.

As IRA craftsmen, we'll build a custom Open Opportunity IRA for you quickly and efficiently, leaving out the guesswork, and handle such details as:

- Judging what state is best for forming the LLC, given what you want to do
- Getting the LLC properly formed under the laws of the right state
- Providing an Operating Agreement that correctly fits an LLC
- Obtaining an EIN for the LLC
- Delivering the LLC into your IRA
- Introducing you to a licensed custodian that understands how to coordinate an LLC with an IRA
- Putting everything together with the custodian

Our relationship won't end once the Open Opportunity IRA is built, though; we'll stick with you to give you the right advice when you need it, and to handle all of the required annual maintenance.

Courtesy of Passport IRA, www.PassPortIRA.com

(*Authors' comment:* For further information, or to enroll in the program, please call: (727) 564-9416 or e-mail: WallSt101@hotmail.com.)

Final Note

Think it can't happen where you live? Think again. Late 2010, the *French government* went through an elaborate process to change its pension laws, "legally" allowing politicians to steal retirement funds from the public in order to pay off other debts.

In the US, public pensions have been raided for years; Congress routinely "borrows" from Social Security to make up budget shortfalls. This is what talking heads mean when they play down concerns of a $14 trillion debt "because we owe it to ourselves"—$4.6 trillion of the debt is owed to intragovernmental agencies like Social Security.

Chances of this money being repaid to Social Security in full? Slim. The trend is more debt, not paying off existing debt. In fact, I'm convinced that politicians have their eyes firmly fixed on the trillions of dollars in private, individual retirement accounts (IRAs) in the United States to fund new spending.

Courtesy of Simon Black

US "Financial Mess" Will Force Government to Take Your Gold!

Economist Marc Faber, publisher of the *Gloom, Boom and Doom* report, says the government will seize privately held gold, even as he continues to buy physical gold himself.

"I prefer to play the commodity space by owning physical gold," Faber tells Chiefsworld. "If I were an American, I would store it outside the US, because in the US, it is not completely unlikely that they will eventually take it away."

"Like in 1933, gold will be purchased back by the government" because eventually the financial mess will be so bad that gold prices "will go ballistic, and the government will take away something from a minority, and not many people own gold."

"When gold prices shoot up, it will be quite a popular measure to take it away from these rich people," Faber says. "It's happened before."

From May 1, 1933, until 1974, US citizens could no longer hold gold as a protection against paper money, which also lost its gold backing at the same time.

Foreign central banks could continue to exchange the US dollars that came into their possession—known as eurodollars for decades—for gold and did so particularly when the US dollar was devalued and then floated against the gold price in 1971.

Faber says he's not in a hurry to buy gold, but accumulates gold every month because he believes the gold market is still under a correction.

Faber notes that the Chinese economy is slowing, and says it will slow further and perhaps crash at some point, which is why he is staying out of commodities other than gold.

Meanwhile, Nomura's Bob Janjuah says markets are so rigged by government policies that investing dangers lurk virtually everywhere.

"My personal recommendation is to sit in gold and non-financial high quality corporate credit and blue-chip big cap non-financial global equities," Janjuah writes at Zero Hedge.

"Bond and currency markets are now so rigged by policy makers that I have no meaningful insights to offer, other than my bubble fears."

Elsewhere, gold traders are getting more bullish after billionaire hedge-fund manager John Paulson told investors it's time to buy the metal as protection against inflation caused by government spending.

Twelve of 22 surveyed by Bloomberg expect prices to gain next week, and five were neutral. Paulson & Co. is already the biggest investor in the SPDR Gold Trust, the largest exchange-traded product backed by bullion, with a stake valued at $2.9 billion, a February 14, 2011 Securities and Exchange Commission filing showed.

Courtesy of Julie Crawshaw, Moneynews

4: UNCLE SAM WANTS YOUR IRAS, 401KS, 403B PLANS, AND GOLD!

Our comment: We agree that desperate governments do desperate things. It is probable that investors may flock to the concept of converting their diminishing IRAs and 401Ks to a safe, 30-year US government annuity program paying 3%, after an "event" or a stock market crash. However, it is our opinion that this is the worst action any American investor could take, as with expected inflation of 20% per year, going forward, a 3% annuity would be virtually valueless in a matter of a few years.

Our action: Monica and I, prior to leaving for NZ, cashed in all of our IRAs, paid the penalties and taxes, and placed the proceeds in gold. Had we known about Passport IRA and the Global Gold Overseas program, we surely would have kept our IRAs and sent them overseas (out of harm's way), and saved the taxes and penalties. Again, knowledge is power—and our main reason for writing this book. So many Americans just listen to their broker, who is, in most cases, bought and paid for by his or her brokerage firm. I know, as I was there for almost 40 years.

CHAPTER FIVE

Capital Controls

"Every government degenerates when trusted to the rulers of the people alone. The people themselves are its only safe depositories."

—Thomas Jefferson

THE COMING BANKING HOLIDAY

Throughout history, governments on the brink of insolvency have routinely enacted similar policies. Sliding into economic obscurity, they'll engage in reckless, cannibalistic initiatives—higher taxes, burdensome regulation, war, destruction of the productive class, etc. It only hastens the end game.

This time is not different. And we can expect more and more of the same. Up next will be new laws that:

- Restrict cash transactions over a certain amount. (Italy has already passed such measures for amounts exceeding 1,000 euros)

- Nationalize pension funds and private retirement accounts. (Again, this has already happened around the world from Ireland to Argentina.)

- Impose a national sales tax and reduce death tax exemptions. (This is already at the forefront of the ongoing tax debate in the US.)

- Ban gold and silver personal holdings. (If you think this can't happen, ask any of the 250,000 people who used to own Liberty Dollar coins before they were seized by the FBI in 2007.)

- And more.

The thing is, every time one of these new bills crops up, there always seems to be a small resistance movement fighting it tooth and nail on the ground. Hence, yesterday's SOPA/PIPA blackout. But ultimately, the political establishment wins.

It›s impossible to shake the public from its apathy...to steer people from the mind-numbing drivel of prime time airwaves... to rescue them from the PSYOPS campaigns of the 24/7 news channels.

5: CAPITAL CONTROLS

We can only take care of ourselves. Any money or energy spent fighting the government or rousing grassroots support is inherently better spent looking after your own interests and making sure that you and your family aren't victims of historical certainty.

And make no mistake; collapse of empire is a historical certainty. From the Babylonians to the Persians to the Romans to the Mayans to the Mongolians to the Ottomans, no empire is built to last. And the final years are anything but smooth sailing.

Courtesy of Simon Black, senior editor, SovereignMan.com

Martin Armstrong Interviewed by Jim Puplava, of Financial Sense News Hour (On Capital Controls)

MP3 Version link (copy & paste in your address bar): www.NetCastDaily.com/broadcast/fsn2012-0105-1.mp3

Jim: Joining me as my special guest on the program today is Martin Armstrong from *ArmstrongEconomics.com,* and Martin, in December of 2010 the US passed the HIRE Act which increased reporting requirements for US citizens holding assets overseas. It would appear to me Martin that step-by-step the government is implementing programs of capital control. Do you see it that way?

Martin: Oh, absolutely! I mean, we're in a situation where the budget deficits are just blowing out, and its going to get much worse. And so what's happening is that instead of dealing with the issues the government is going to be much more aggressive to tax people, chase them down, put them in prison. All kinds of crazy stuff. This new act that came in December 19th, effectively they are telling any foreign corporation that they must report any activity with an American overseas. And what they're going to do to them is what they did to UBS. If they don't comply, they will confiscate all their assets here. So, honestly, from an international perspective, the best advice I could tell people is that, is to get out. If you're going to do business in the United States use an agent. Get your branches out of this country. It's going to get far worse.

Jim: It would almost appear, this is something that happened in Germany under the Nazis, where they began to collect and find out where the assets were, and eventually, as we know in the case of the Jews, they confiscated them. But it seems like, whenever you have a government that is trying to keep tabs of what you're doing, what you own, where it's held…that's a government that's intent on taking some of it.

Martin: Yeah, I mean this is, you know the slogans tend to really mask the truth. And that is, "The rich don't pay their fair share", etc. What this is really about is that only the United States and Japan tax worldwide income. So, if you're parents were American and you happen to be born in Kenya or something, and you never come back to this country, you still owe taxes to the United States. So, it's not a question of paying your fair share. An American is basically, when he's born, is an economic slave. And you owe money to this country, whether you're here, whether you receive any of the benefits or not. Whereas Europeans, they pay if you use the services. If you're going to stay in the country, then you pay taxes. A "Brit" who works in Hong Kong, doesn't pay taxes back in Britain. He pays his taxes in Hong Kong. Americans have to pay in both places. So, it's one of the primary reasons why also, US companies are forced offshore, which the government doesn't like to talk about.

5: CAPITAL CONTROLS

But, for example, the Yellow River Dam in China, not one American company got any of the construction. Why? Because German companies were already 33% cheaper bidding on the same project than an American company. And, because they earn the money outside the country, it's tax free. Americans don't. So we really cannot compete on a global scale, which is one of the primary reasons why companies leave. And of course they don't want to talk about that. You know, that's the reality of what we're facing here.

Jim: You know, throughout history, governments rarely reform themselves. In fact, when you look at the Roman Empire, England under Charles I, France during the French Revolution, it seems like the powers of the State, as the State's debts expand, the powers of the State against the people also grow. Is this likely to happen here? I mean, it seems like, little by little, that's what's happening. Our rights, and the Constitution, the Bill of Rights, are being stripped away from us almost on an annual basis.

Martin: Well, essentially, the Bill of Rights is gutted already. There's nothing left. If, you know, just take the very simple thing, the rights, Freedom of Speech and Freedom of Assembly. OK, I mean, you can look at what they did basically to the "Occupy Wall Street" people. Regardless if you agree or disagree with them. I mean they basically arrest them. They say "Oh, you're walking on the grass", or they say "You're violating…" "Well, we're really not violating your First Amendment Rights," you violated some other minor statute over here. So, this is how they get around everything. Ah, they always, I think it was, I just saw on the Internet that 40,000 new laws are being proposed for 2012 already. (Chuckle.) I mean, this is crazy. We have, I mean, God did the Ten Commandments, man did about 10 billion laws. (Laugh.) So, and we're trying to say the same thing countless times. I mean over and over again. The Bill of Rights is gone.

That's completely finished. And there is no question that somebody can actually protest, permit, and all this other kind of stuff. Now that's all out the window.

And, you can go pretty much down the line. Forth Amendment…gone. The Fifth Amendment…they basically have held that you're right to remain silent, that's only personal. If you work for a company, which basically 99% of the people do, you don't have such a right because Corporations don't have such rights. I mean, you go right down the line. You look at this new bill that they just put in, that the military can operate domestically; deny people counsel, lock them up—citizens now—alright. No right to go to court, no right to lawyers, no right to a trial. They can just hold you indefinitely until you die. And all under the pretense, "oh, it's terrorism." Well, how do you know somebody is a terrorist? You know, you have to have a right to what its [sic] called, due process of law.

And due process of law actually comes from the Bible, and it comes from Genesis. When God basically says to Cain, "Where is your brother?" He already knows supposedly what happened. But He's giving him the right. He's summoning him and He's giving him the right to be heard. That is the fundamental principle of due process of law. And this new bill says that you do not have that. That we can just lock you up; you have no right to lawyers, no right to a judge, no right to a public trial, no right to even find out what they say against you. Nothing. So, we're about the closest we can get to Nazism.

Jim: Well, on another issue, too, which is maybe why the government is doing this. We're seeing world economies start to crumble under their burdens of debt, and yet the governments' response is to expand government. And the US has gone from 18% of GDP on its' way to 25%. We've seen increased regulations, and you just talked about numerous bills being proposed for this year. And as they increase these regs and the size of government, taxation and regulation are strangling the economies. So instead of lowering taxes and reducing the size of government, they're going in the opposite direction. Government is getting more rapacious in terms of its demands on its citizens.

Martin: This is exactly how Rome collapsed. There was a Roman Emperor, Maximinus in 238 [AD], he simply declared all wealth in the Roman Empire to be his. That's it. And, what happened, is that, and what you're going to see over the next few years, as you attack the rich, as the Romans did, what happens is that, somebody now hoards their money. They no longer invest it, they hide it, and they don't keep it in banks. And consequently, that reduces the velocity of money. And as it reduces the velocity that is what creates the economic decline. So that interest rates, even during the Great Depression, fell to 1%, nobody would borrow because they didn't see an opportunity to make money. And every possible mistake that every government has made before us, we are following step by step.

I mean you take the 2007 crisis. There were over ten agencies regulating these CDOs. Not a single one was able to do anything. You look at MF Global. It's blown up, they stole almost basically two billion dollars from people; the clearing exchange hasn't honored it. Nobody will do anything about it. The FTC, I mean, we have all these regulators. What have they ever prevented? Nothing! Absolutely nothing! And it's just a real giant joke. And the other problem that we are now facing and why government is rising exponentially is that as the baby boomers retire, this is also happening with government employees. So now they have to pay them virtually 100% of what they've been earning the last three years. Now they have to go out and hire somebody else to replace them. So the cost of government on the retirees is basically doubling. And there is no way out of this without some sort of honest reform. And government is not about to do it because, largely I think…. Well, historically you're asking them…they have to give up power, which they are not going to do.

And additionally, we really don't have a democracy, per se. You saw politicians stand up and say, "Oh Saddam Hussein was a dictator, and Gaddafi. Oh, they've been in power for thirty years." Then you look at these senators and you say, "Well how long have you been down there?" About the same amount of time. You know, we really don't have choices and whoever is sponsored by the party has to basically kowtow to the party. So, you know it's very rare to find an individual like Ron Paul, for example, but the press tries to ignore him desperately. Why? Because he's not really part of the mainstream.

So, I don't see where we have any hope of doing anything, and because [of] the politicians. We need term limits desperately. It is unfortunately…I mean even if you want to, say a Congressman, increase the term to four years, fine. But one time—that's it—out and gone!

I mean, I don't care who you put in as president, Obama is already spending the last, almost half the term that he's in for, preparing to get elected for the second time. So, you know, it should be one time only for everybody. And then, they›re actually, maybe going to do something that they should be doing without having to say, "Well gee, I had better not vote on this because I am going to get elected and nobody likes that."

You know, without serious political reform, I mean we're just really screwed. Totally!

Jim: This brings up the question of what has been referred to as the Fourth Estate. That would appear, Martin, that we no longer

5: CAPITAL CONTROLS

operate in this country with a free press. In fact I would probably call it the government media. Because its views, its readership is declining because of its bias and slant of how issues are presented to the public, or how issues are ignored. And that's the tragedy here because our Founding Fathers always believed in a free press and the freedom of speech, that the media would be a check on government. Instead they've become another arm of government. Isn't that another problem that we face here?

Martin: Yeah, there's just…the press is absolutely terrible. Ah, I mean, it's been going on for a while. When Michael Milken back in 1987, he was going to go to trial. Then they finally forced him into pleading. And not one American paper told the truth. The only paper that reported the full true story was the *London Financial Times.* Michael Milken, they first charged his brother, trying to force him to plead guilty. His brother said, "Don't worry about it, let's go to trial." Then they went after his 90 year old grandfather, and said, "If you don't plead guilty, we're going to charge him."

So, I mean not one of the American papers won't ever tell the truth about anything here. I mean it's an absolute joke. We have a conviction rate in this country that is 10% higher than Adolph Hitler. I mean that's alarming. The only person we haven't beaten is Stalin, and that's only because he basically said, "Take everybody away." But I mean the most notorious court of Adolph Hitler had a conviction rate of 90%. We're at 99! I mean, what does that tell you? The federal government can never be wrong about anybody at any time. So it really gets to be scary.

Jim: I want to move on to another issue that is confronting the markets, not only last year, but looks like a carryover into this year. And that is the sovereign debt crisis. We've seen in Europe the December 9th agreement to cede sovereignty. I guess, as you look at this crisis unfold, do you believe that Germany will stick to its hard line or will the politicians and bureaucrats, in order to preserve the Euro, will Germany blink, if it means saving the Euro in the end?

Martin: According to very high sources I have in Germany, if the choice comes between the collapse of the Euro or blinking and letting inflation take place, they will take the latter. They have so much invested in this Euro its pathetic that, there too, they simply will not do the right thing.

I mean, as a trader, I warned them back in '97. If you're going to leave every country with its own individual bond, if you short the bond you basically have a virtual currency. Its just a derivative, that's it. The only way to have actually created a single currency was, like the United States, you have to create a single national debt. Can you imagine what the national debt of this country would be if all fifty states had the right to issue federal debt? I mean it would be total chaos. But that's what Europe has got. And largely because the politicians…I mean the two words that should have been divorced the minute they met are "political economy." Because, they don't know what they're doing… most of them are lawyers. And they have done a fantastic job of always screwing up everything, every step of the way. And Europe, unfortunately is in the same boat. And they…it's gotten worse now. Where before you thought Greece was in bad shape you sold the currency. It actually devalued the debt. Now what happens is, because the currency is the Euro, you have to sell the bonds. So you sell the bonds, and what happens is the interest rates don't go up. What we're really facing this year is, and remarkably no one is talking about it yet, there is six hundred (600) billion Euros that have to be rolled, and that is just Spain and Italy this year. You're rolling from interest rates that are 1.5% to 2%, to 7%. So everywhere we look the national

5: CAPITAL CONTROLS

debt of everyone around is going to go exponentially higher. So this is why the countries are getting very aggressive with their taxation. I believe that historically you're going to see more and more people hoard money and not really invest. It's just everything they could possibly do wrong they are doing.

Jim: Well, you know we've seen, Martin, a lot of protests. Whether we've seen it here in the states, Greece, the Middle East... And governments I would think would have to look with trepidation at events in the Middle East where a rebellion used social media to bring the rebellion together and to get organized. There is a recent bill that was introduced into the Senate by Senator Joseph Lieberman and Susan Collins; it's called "protecting cyber space."

Shouldn't that also be a warning in terms of the steps government is taking? And it seems like, Martin, they sort of have a sense that this is coming. In other words, people will only sit back and be a slave for so long before the slaves revolt.

Martin: Oh, yeah, they know it. They proposed that within months of what happened in the Middle East. And I'm a programmer. You cannot attack every server in this country simultaneously. You can maybe attack one server; you know you can attack the government. You can unplug those, but you cannot unplug the entire internet. And this is what the president now... That's what they want the power to do. Which will basically shut down all the social media. But it will also shut down where the free press is. Everybody turns to the Internet for radio, for all these things. This will all be shut off in the blink of an eye if the government just doesn't like it. And they can always now claim, "Oh, its some terrorist." I mean these nineteen guys and a camel have taken away all our rights, where World War I, Korea, Vietnam...none of those standing armies could have done what nineteen guys and a camel did.

THE COMING BANKING HOLIDAY

Jim: I want to move on to something that we're seeing play out in the economy, and I'd like to get your explanation for our listeners.

On one hand we have two opposing forces at work. We have deleveraging taking place in the private sector, and we've seen that steadily since the crisis in 2007. And yet we have monetary and fiscal expansion on the side of the government, which is inflationary. So it seems like, Martin, we have a battle between the forces of inflation and deflation occurring simultaneously. And looking at the economic numbers and even the inflation rate, what we've got in its place is stagflation.

Martin: Yes. Its [sic] hard to get a full bead on the full amount of deflation we're going through. I would put it at a very bear minimum of 15 trillion dollars. And that is the lowering of asset values across the board. So, if you look at just the real estate market, the outstanding mortgages were about 15 trillion. So, if you really just want to look at that, there's a third off of that, so you're talking five trillion dollars. So the Feds increasing the monetary supply through its elastic facility, you're talking about a little less than three trillion dollars. That's why there was no real inflation. QE 1 and 2 really did not stimulate. They can't pump in enough money to basically fix it the way they've done. What they should have done, which would have been much simpler, was to forget their friends and relatives in the banking industry. They should have just taken all the mortgages across the board and just said OK, fine, we're chopping them by 25% and let the government pay up for that. That would have done a heck of a lot more for the economy because, number one, it would have prevented all these massive foreclosures, which essentially affects everybody.

Because what happens is so much housing comes on the market that your house, even if you are fully paid up, depreciates in

5: CAPITAL CONTROLS

value because of the supply that's out there to be sold. And the banks have absolutely done a terrible job at this. They didn't have...pay attention really to what they were doing. They started pooling all these mortgages together. And I can tell you that anybody that had any kind of a problem with not being able to pay their mortgage or whatever, all they really have to do is say, you want...if somebody tries to foreclose, "Give me the certified copy of the mortgage." Because once they pooled these things and they sliced them and diced them, no one actually knew who actually owned what. So that's why you have some people being able to stay in houses for three years. You know, they're getting basically rent-free and whatever, largely because they pooled these things together that should never have been done. And they go to the government with their hat in hand and ask for, you know, 700 billion dollars to bail themselves out. Not the economy. That hasn't done anything for anybody, other than make the bankers rich again, that's about it.

Jim: You know, as we look at these opposing forces that we've been talking about here, inflation, deflation. This leads me to gold and how it has performed. In September, Martin, it looked like...as it crossed over 1900 it was on its way to 2000. Instead, it ended the year below 1600. Now, you believe the market has the possibility, in the gold market, to retest the 1225–1325 area going into this year. What would be the catalyst for this move downward in your opinion?

Martin: It's largely this battle between inflation and deflation. I don't see the inflationary pressure currently. We're still burdened more with a deflationary contraction still. But that will probably start to, I would think reverse, this summer. After the summer it will start to percolate back upward in the inflationary side. Largely because we have so much debt rolling over that the interest expenditures are going to go up in Europe and elsewhere. And I think that we're going to see that a lot more capital tends to be hoarded, and if you're going to be looking at hoarding cash at this time you certainly don't want to do it in cash in a bank, per se. So I do think that people will tend to look a little bit more at the metals, particularly gold, later on in 2012. More in the second half.

So I think that we're going to have to really be concerned about how the government is moving in every single direction here with taxation, with cutting off the Internet, with authorizing domestic activity with the military. All this is pointing in one direction that they know that they have trouble coming. And, historically, even with Fascism or whatever appears in Europe, it just takes one or two years for it to pop up over here. So, the other thing that we really have a problem with, which is similar to the Great Depression, is that…people don't realize is that you really have to pay attention to what was the unemployment at that point in time. Unemployment was really about what it is today. It really only went up to slightly under ten percent from the financial market side. What came in as a second punch and drove unemployment to 25 percent was largely after the lows were in place going into 1935, etc.

The reason for that was the Dust Bowl and 40% of the civil workforce at the time, were farmers. And you could not pass a law to make it rain. So it was the final stage of the Industrial Revolution that forced people out of the agricultural sector and into becoming skilled labor. So by the time you get to 1980 the agricultural sector is only eight percent. We're in the same similar situation today, except for that 40 percent figure of the civil workforce is employed by government. And this is a bit worse in the sense that they do not really contribute anything to economic growth. That's why we call them public servants. It's like hiring a maid in your house, that's very nice, but she's going to cost

5: CAPITAL CONTROLS

you money…she's not making it so that you can earn more. And a public servant is basically the same thing. It's a cost of living. Although the government doesn't put it in the CPI indexes, it is part of our cost of living. And 40 per cent of the civil workforce is employed by the government.

So as government is rising in cost exponentially this is our great problem. Because the state and local governments are going to be forced into more and more layoffs, etc., because they can't print money like the Feds can. So, you're going to see more bankruptcies, etc. So, the unemployment we see going forward is largely going to be coming from the public sector rather than the private sector. And, uh, unemployment is going to go up rather significantly. And its a part of the process we have to go through. We have to get…reduce the size of government, make it more efficient again. I said, you had over ten agencies regulating the CDOs and nobody did the job. I mean, one would be, that actually functioned, would be far better than more than ten that do nothing.

Jim: You know one of the things that I've noticed in your writings Martin, is that you make a lot of references to the Roman Empire. And like yourself, I am a student of Roman history. If you were to recommend something on Rome that our listeners could read that would give them sort of some insights because we seem to be running parallel to many of the things that caused the eventual decline of the Roman Empire. What book would you read? Would you recommend Gibbons?

Martin: Well, Gibbons is probably one of the better ones. But it, it has maybe a bit of a bias in it as far as religion is concerned. He was fairly oppressed by religion, and when you read it, you have to keep in mind that this was also coming out of the period of the great religious wars in England between the Catholics and the Protestants. So, he tended to look at things a little bit more religiously, giving it much more credence that it was worth. I'm trying to finish a book on it to really bring it together from a lot of different sources. There is no one particular source that I could tell you. But I think what Gibbons missed on the religious side was that the real conversion to Christianity only came when the economy collapsed. So that people were praying to their various different gods and nothing happened. And that is really when they turned to Christianity, and that is in the third century. So that when you have Constantine basically in battle, he's marching forward under the sign of the cross, etc. So that is really where the major persecutions took place and where the big shift in religious values take place. And that really was driven by the economy more than anything else at that stage. That's where you get the big surge.

Prior to that, Christianity still very much, was a minor type sect. The persecutions began largely because Nero was the first one do to it, and he basically wanted to blame them (the Christians) instead of himself for setting fire to Rome.

Jim: So is there any, outside of Gibbons, outside that bias, is there any book that you've read personally that had an impact in your thinking?

Martin: Well, I would say, you know, Adam Smith really, his *Wealth of Nations.* I think really is probably the beginning and the end in economics. That it's fairly simple and straightforward and that is that everybody operates under their own self interest. And that not only applies personally to various different individuals, but also to government. So, that's why Communism failed, because it sounds nice, you create government and you hand them…you take all the toys away from the rich, but, so all you did was take them from one party and place them in the hands

5: CAPITAL CONTROLS

of another and then that was power, and they didn't want to give that up. (Chuckle.) You can't get away from this self-interest. It doesn't matter who it is. It's our problem with government right now as we've been talking, and it's going to get much more aggressive in taxation. Because its self-interest is to survive, it will not reform willingly at any point in time. It has just never happened. So when you get to these points in history where the debt is always what destroys every society going back to 6,000 BC.

And there were debt crises that Aristotle wrote about. So this is nothing new. It's the same thing all the time. There were real estate speculations in Athens. He talked about how real estate collapsed. So it's hard for me to point you to one particular book. I mean I've read so many different things, that I would say that the self-interest concept by Adam Smith is probably by far the best overview; and then there are a lot of different books that I've read on specific periods. So the one I'm trying to write now is to try and gather all that together and bring it into one place so that you can actually look at Athens, and etc., in comparison.

Jim: Well, when that book is complete, please, give me a heads up because I would love to have you on the program to discuss it.

Martin, as we close, give out your website, because you publish a lot of good information that you make available to the public free. And, but also, you are going to be cranking up the computer modeling in terms of forecasting, which will be a subscription service. Spend a moment if you would as we close and tell our listeners about that.

Martin: Well, we began as a public service providing information, historical comparisons and things of this nature, and details as to what is happening politically on a global scale. And just as we were talking about the press, our readership is now is over 500,000, and we provide it all free as a public service.

And I mean the *New York Times,* to put it into comparison, has a circulation of 800,000. We're pretty large on an international scale at this point. And it is mainly provided to give people the sources where to actually find a lot of these different things and what is actually truly happening. And that you can get at "armstrongeconomics.com" or "martinarmstrong.org", and they're provided.... You know you can go on there and pull down reports that are written for the last several years. That's all provided for free. So we have a lot of students who are always using it...things of that nature. And it's translated into different languages. So its been very very good, for a lot of people over this chaotic period of time.

Jim: Well, keep up the good work, Martin. As always it's a pleasure to be speaking with you. I want to wish you a healthy and prosperous New Year. And once again if you want to follow Martin's work, just go to "armstrongeconomics.com," that's "armstrongeconomics.com" or "armstrongeconomics.org."

And we've been speaking with the head of Armstrong Economics, Martin Armstrong. Martin, thanks so much for joining us on the program.

Martin: Thank you very much for inviting me.

Courtesy of Jim Puplava, Financial Sense News Hour

5: CAPITAL CONTROLS

Our comment: As they say, it's not a question of *if,* but *when* capital controls are going to be imposed on Americans. When countries become financially exhausted, historically, they impose capital controls on their citizens. And as the chapter mentions, you can always send your money and investments back to America if capital controls are imposed, but you can't do it the other way around. Better safe than sorry, as we used to say in Hawaii. And, it costs you nothing!

Our action: We brought our investments and savings here to NZ, and our gold to Switzerland.

CHAPTER SIX

A Look at a Suisse Precious Metals Depository

"You have a choice between the natural stability of gold and the honesty and intelligence of the members of government. And with all due respect for those gentlemen, I advise you, as long as the capitalist system lasts, vote for gold."

—George Bernard Shaw

Where Are Your Real Assets in Times of Economic and Political Uncertainty?

It is becoming increasingly obvious to investors worldwide that most traditional investments are not as safe or reliable as they once were. If that wasn't enough, the US dollar is suffering the predictable consequences of the unrestrained expansion of our money supply. Both economics and history teach us that the dollar's value must decrease, while the prices of goods and services must increase. The only thing that we can be sure of from the greatest expansion of the money supply in US history is the greatest subsequent inflation rate in US history. Not surprisingly gold continues to rise as investors recognize the seriousness of the current situation. The Obama administration will likely make a number of economic mistakes that will cost us dearly. We expect higher taxes on payrolls, income, capital gains, property, and inheritances.

We expect restrictions on currency exchanges. We also expect restrictions on the amount of money you can move in and out of the country. In other words, we expect a further loss of our personal, economic, and perhaps even religious freedoms. So what do we do?

One of the most practical decisions that an investor can make is to safeguard some assets by moving them overseas. To many, this may seem like an overwhelming or daunting task, but believe me, the idea of owning assets outside the US has moved from exotic to mainstream.

In fact, we can no longer afford to ignore the very real threats to our liberties here in the US. As the consequences of the moral and economic decline in America are felt, the US Government will move to protect itself at the expense of its citizens.

6: A LOOK AT A SUISSE PRECIOUS METALS DEPOSITORY

Let's explore where to buy gold overseas, and then hear from a quality Suisse Gold Depository expert, tell us about "his" company.

Where to Buy Our Gold?

The first question was "WHERE?" It didn't take us long to decide on Switzerland. No country has a longer history (over 300 years) of being a safe-haven in time of crisis.

The second question was "WHAT?" Again, it didn't take us long to decide. What better or more reliable asset is there than gold. (And now all of the precious metals are available)

"HOW?" was the final challenge, but even that has turned out to be easier than expected. In fact, it is so convenient that investing overseas is just as easy as purchasing gold here in the US

Advantages of Having Precious Metals in Switzerland

- Restrictions on, or even possible confiscation of, gold and other tangible assets.
- Restrictions on funds coming into and going out of the US (currency exchange controls, wire limitations, etc.).
- Heavier and more oppressive taxation in the US
- An even more socialist government and society.
- Restrictions on international travel (Homeland Security, passports, threat of terrorism, TSA, etc.)
- Greater limitations and restrictions on the use of your US property.

Some of the Gold & Silver Coins You Can Buy from a Suisse Based Depository:

GOLD
- 100g Bar
- 250g Bar
- 500g Bar
- 1000g Bar (1kg)
- 1oz S.A. Krugerrand
- 1oz Austrian Philharmonic
- 1oz Canadian Maple Leaf
- 1oz American Eagle

SILVER
- 1000g Bar (1kg)
- 5000g Bar (5kg)
- 15000g Bar (15kg)
- 1oz Austrian Philharmonic
- 1oz Canadian Maple Leaf
- 1oz American Eagle

PLATINUM
- 100g Bar
- 1000g Bar (1kg)

PALLADIUM
- 100g Bar
- 1000g Bar (1kg)

6: A LOOK AT A SUISSE PRECIOUS METALS DEPOSITORY

What to Look for When Choosing a Suisse Precious Metals Depository

- Physically allocated and directly owned—nothing less!
- Direct and unencumbered ownership of physically allocated gold, silver, platinum, and palladium products.
- No paper metal solutions (certificates etc.)
- Client's metals must not be exposed to creditor obligations, or counter party risks.
- They cannot be pledged, leased or otherwise disposed of without the client's explicit instructions.

A company that appears to meet these criteria is Global Gold. Here's a 2/11/2012 interview with Claudio Grass, managing director of the precious metals division of the company.

*"It's not **if**, but **when**."*

"...gold and economic freedom are inseparable. In the absence of the gold standard, there is no way to protect savings from confiscation through inflation. Gold stands as the protector of property rights. If one grasps this, one has no difficulty in understanding the statists antagonism toward the gold standard."

—Alan Greenspan, *"Gold and Economic Freedom"* in Capitalism: The Unknown Ideal. *Ayn Rand, ed., (New York: New American Library, 1967), p.96*

Mr. Grass, you are the Managing Director of the Precious Metals division of Global Gold. Can you tell us a bit more about your company?

Global Gold Inc., was founded in 2008 and is specialized in the purchase and storage of gold, silver, platinum, and palladium. As a subsidiary of BFI Capital Group AG, Global Gold benefits from a long history, impeccable track record and vast experience in the realm of wealth management, financial services and precious metal investments. Our parent company is a Swiss wealth management group that has been in business since 1991, overseeing more than US$2 billion in total client assets and with more than US$250 million of assets under discretionary management. Global Gold has quickly grown into an internationally recognized and respected physical precious metals storage programs.

You are one of the keynote speakers on our forthcoming conference about the tragedy of the Euro. Can you comment on the recent developments in Europe? Is the Euro really going to crash?

I personally believe that the question is not if, but when. When we look at the actual currency war, it is obvious, that this is not the crisis of one currency, but the crisis of a whole fiat money system. History tells us that there is a clear connection between Hyperinflation and the paper currency system, and it is also a fact that almost every Hyperinflation happened in the twenties century. The only Hyperinflation before happened during the French revolution, when their monetary system was also based on a paper currency standard. Since 1971, when President Nixon closed the Gold Window, the actual monetary system is backed by nothing but trust, representing the longest fiat money or paper standard system ever. Therefore the risk that history repeats itself is definitely given.

But we are going to pay our coffee with it, aren't we?

6: A LOOK AT A SUISSE PRECIOUS METALS DEPOSITORY

That is true. But for how long? The paper we used as money used to be a property title, now it is a debt security. Our paper money has transformed from I-owe-something to I-owe-you. It is nothing more but collateral, and a special form of collateral: the promise of the former generation that future generation will pay of the debt.

For forty years, the world has operated on a debt-based monetary system which is fueled by means of credit creation. It stands or falls on the assumption that the debt upon which it is based will, someday, be repaid. For a long time, that was not a problem, because money and debt creation follows the exponential growth function.

The best example to explain exponential growth I have heard of so far came from Chris Martenson and he describes it as follows:

"You go to the bank to get your first loan for 1000 Euros. At this time the bank has an asset, which is your loan on the books. You own 1000 Euros in cash and a liability of 1000 Euros towards the bank. Let's say after one month, when you have to pay the first interest we see 1000 Euros in money still exist in circulation but your dept has grown by the size of the interest, for example 10 Euros. Now you own the bank a total depth of 1010 Euros in total. So where does the 10 Euros coming from because there are only 1000 Euros in money available? It must loaned into existence, in the form of 10 Euros of new money plus 10 Euros of debt that must also be paid back with interest."

Therefore this process rises for a long time very moderately. You hardly even notice it. But then, all of the sudden, there is a massive acceleration, and then the point of no return is long gone. It is only a matter of time before people start to realize that. This is why Global Gold has been founded a couple of years ago: we know that there is a huge market for people who are looking exactly for this kind of security. Our product fits like a glove: a safe storage for gold and silver, managed by people with experience.

Ok, so gold and silver. But why would that be such a safe haven? Hasn't gold gone up so much already? I am playing the devils' advocate of course, I know the answer already.

I know. Especially people that have read Mises and Rothbard no longer let themselves be fooled on these matters. Gold has not risen in value, not even a bit. It is the way you measure its worth that has changed. Let me give you an example. Two thousand years ago, one ounce of Gold bought you a nice "Roman Tunica," and today nothing has changed: I could take you to a place here in Geneva where you can buy a tailor-made suit that equals the dignity of a Roman senator, and it still costs you one ounce of gold. So, to conclude: gold does not rise in value, it is the euro that lose it. The more money printed, the more fiat paper money depreciates against gold.

Got it. Now the only thing to do is to convince the rest of the world.

I hear you. Most people use the word "gold" in every day verbiage, but if you tell them that we might face a high inflation and that they should buy some gold, they look like you are from another planet. They simply do not get the historical value of gold anymore. But its history is very interesting. Gold and silver became money because they have all the intrinsic characteristics of being a good medium of exchange: durable, homogeneous in quality, recognizable, scarce, and lots of other qualities. Out of all the possible means of indirect exchange—cattle, barley, salt, you name it—gold and silver got selected by the market for thousands of years. People should really think about that.

6: A LOOK AT A SUISSE PRECIOUS METALS DEPOSITORY

Ok, let's talk more about that at the conference. For the time being, I am more interested in how your product actually works. Let's say I want to buy gold with Global Gold. How does that work in practice?

Signing up for an account is relatively simple. The most important thing is that we know our customers and understand their background of assets and thus, we ask for a clear identification. In this context I'd like to mention that Global Gold is a registered member of VQF, a vocational organization of Swiss asset managers and financial services institutions, supervised by the Swiss Financial Market Supervisory Authority with the objective of quality assurance according to professional standards and Swiss law.

What would be the next step then?

After the registration procedure is completed, you are homefree, and it all is quite simple. You just wire the money you want to put into gold and silver, and you place your order. Your order can executed during one of Global Gold's two daily trading hours: between 09–10 AM or 16–17 PM Central European Time. And when the purchase is made, and the metal is in the vault, you will receive in both cases notice.

I am willing to believe that, but let's stay sharp. How am I sure that my gold is really there? And what happens if you guys go broke?

"Read the small letters", we always say. Buying gold nowadays is not a problem anymore, but are you actually buying gold? A rapidly growing number of precious metal certificates, ETFs and other "paper metal" solutions, generally issued by banks, are being introduced to the market. But most of these have provisions that protect the interests of the issuer in the context of a crisis. Generally, when you read those contracts, it stipulates that when "unusual market conditions" arise, the issuers have the right to suspend transactions in the product.

Well, well. But who reads those contracts anyway?

Exactly. And what are "unusual market conditions"? The crash of a currency? And even if people the "Terms of a Agreement," they often don't know what to look for. How many people actually know what a "cash settlement clause" is? If you agree to such a contract, the issuers of this "papergold" have the right to pay you out in fiat paper money, and not in the gold you requested. When the proverbial excrement hits the fan, you are a sitting duck. If you you find such a clause, you are sure that you are not buying gold, but a half-promise to gold.

Don't let yourself be fooled! The Global Gold Program does not have any such provisions or cash settlement clauses. It is not a "paper metal" solution. It is the real hold-it-in-your-hand-thing. Our clients are the direct and unencumbered owners of the coins and bars they have bought with us. Your precious metals are not exposed to our creditor obligations, nor are they encumbered with counterparty risks. What we offer is a deposit-contract. Your gold cannot be used as a collateral for loans, nor do we loan it out, or anything else. The only thing we do, is keep it safe for you until you come and get it. It's yours, and nobody else's.

That is starting to look like it.

And what is more: since we have stored your coins and bars one-to-one like you have bought them a request for physical delivery can be effectuated without delay. With Global Gold you do not have to wait for the fabrication of your goods, nor are you subject to any of the related fabrication costs. Your goods are already fabricated and at your immediate disposal. They are in the vault, waiting for you. As a client of Global Gold, you can sell or have your precious metals delivered promptly, even during a financial crisis. I strongly believe that our solution is one of the best products on the market, it is safe and reliable, even during the most harsh crisis scenario's.

Yes, but what in case that Global Gold goes bankrupt? You aren't evading my question, aren't you?

(Laughs.) No, I am not! You Flemings seem to be born suspicious! But that is a good attitude. Let me say loud and clear: we do not own your gold. We provide a brokerage service to buy or sell it, and we store it for you. So, in the event that we go broke, our creditors will not be able to put a claim on your metals. Your metals are not listed on our balance sheet. I hope I have made myself absolutely clear now? (Laughs.)

Yes you have. But there is another thing that worries me. Safety has two dimensions: physical and political. I trust that the gold is stored safely, but I still have concerns about the judicial status of Switzerland. It seems to me that it has lost a lot of its former strength as a jurisdiction where property rights are honored. How do we know that the gold will not be nationalized like they did in the States in 1931?

It is correct that Switzerland has been under attack by almost every foreign government in the last couple of years. Frankly, I expect that as long as the debt and deficits in the other European countries around continue to grow, the pressure on Switzerland will even grow larger. But Switzerland has a long-standing tradition of direct democracy within a federalist structure, and a strong link to gold within the Swiss population, so we consider the risk of a gold confiscation through the political system as very unlikely.

I can understand the doubts and worries people have, but one has to see things in perspective. There are only two things absolutely sure in life: death and taxes. But if there is one place in the world where gold faces a very small chance of being nationalized, it really is Switzerland. Look at all those other jurisdictions that are called safe: either they are part of a geopolitical bargain, with a huge counterparty risk. Or they have a very centralized political structure, which makes it easy to implement new laws without even asking the people. Switzerland is one of the most decentralized nations in the world, has a freedom loving populace, and a solvency that stands out from the rest. Try to pressure that.

Ok, convincing. Now, what does it cost to store gold with you, and what is the lowest amount one can buy?

The minimum investment to become a client is 50000 Swiss Francs. That is about 41000 Euro's now. So even if you have as little 30 Krugerrands, you might consider taking an account with us.

Not exactly the solution for a small investor.

What is a small investor? We believe international diversification doesn't make sense, financial wise, for an individual which has less than 50000 CHF of savings. In such a case you can buy a few Krugerrands and store them in several ways. You can bury them in your garden, or keep them in the attic, or even in your sugar bowl in the kitchen. The only thing I would advise against for people that have more gold than that, is to buy a safe, and put it in there. Don't forget that storing gold at home can be dangerous, especially when you consider that due to growing poverty, criminality will rise. In times of despair, people are afraid of nothing. I personally know stories of people that have been put a gun to their head while they were sleeping. At that point, your safe does not help you anymore, since if you value life, you will give the code of it immediately. But your life savings are gone.

What you need is professional storage, and that, of course, comes with a price. But I dare to say that even here Global Gold is very reasonable with its price setting, and certainly when you take into account the service you get. Global Gold offers physical precious metals in coins and bars at wholesale terms. You can buy the most liquid and famous coins: Krugers, Eagles, Maples, Kangaroos, you name it. If you visit our website, you will see that the prices are updated every 30 seconds, and that they are sharp. We go out and buy those goods for you, and put them in our safe.

The cost?

The main cost to pay is the annual storage fee, because we are a storage company. The fee is based on the amount of gold you store with us. The highest fee (0.7%) is for storages with a value between 50000 CHF–100000 CHF, but that percentage drops sharply when storing more. The lowest fee is as low as 0.4%. The storage fees are invoiced annually in arrears. They are calculated on a pro rata basis and the average value of the precious metals in storage during the respective invoicing period. Don't forget that the storage fee also covers the cost for the insurance of your metals and for the yearly external audit, which is being conducted by an internationally recognized audit partner.

And of course, to cover the cost of us buying the gold for you and actually putting it in the safe, a transaction fee applies. Global Gold does not trade paper, but really goes out in the free market to purchase the physical gold for you. Besides our highly customer oriented services, we also provide the logistic services, by bringing it to the vault, registering it to your name, and doing the reverse when you decide to sell, these are all costs that have to be covered.

Cut the promo. How much?

Ha-ha, you really like to get down to business fast, do you? No problem. The brokerage fee is based on a sliding scale model, which is limited up to 3% on purchases and no more than 1.5% on sales. All fees are transparently agreed to in advance, and will be reported in your transaction statements.

Any other advice?

Yes and no. I cannot say much about that. The only thing I want to stress is that investing is not only about return, but also about risk. I don't think people actually realize the risks they are taking in today's stock markets. Do they take into account that one of the main reason most stocks are still surging higher is because they are being propped up by the ongoing injection of newly created money? In Zimbabwe's stock market, everybody used to be a millionaire until the last reform, when the Reserve Bank of Zimbabwe removed 12 zeros from the currency. The same goes for the euro: governments have been taking on so much debt that it is mathematically impossible ever to repay it. As in our present monetary system debts are magically converted into money, the situation is getting riskier with each bailout.

So the question your customers have to ask themselves is this: "How do you want to protect your wealth and where do you want to store it?" Do you prefer to be invested in an asset that has shown to be rock solid in every crisis during the last 3000 years? People who think that gold is a bubble, do not understand how bubbles come about: you cannot print gold, you can only mine it. Gold is the money of the free market. And mining money costs money too. That is why gold is such a safe haven: whatever the government does, it cannot destroy the intrinsic value of gold, nor can it influence its production. It is stable as a rock.

6: A LOOK AT A SUISSE PRECIOUS METALS DEPOSITORY

The other important question you have to ask is: "Does it make sense to keep some assets outside of the country you live"? When I see how Governments around the world are running into fiscal problems and are setting off on an aggressive hunt for tax money, increasingly employing methods that are at the limit, if not beyond, legality, it makes me really worried. So if your government acts 'above the law', it is time for serious planning. In the absence of rule of law, the most fundamental prerequisite of a functioning free country is undermined. At that stage, protecting your freedom and your property within that country becomes a gamble. Privacy and property are in jeopardy and need to be protected OUTSIDE of your country.

Ok, thank you. Since it seems that I have run out of nasty questions, I suppose we have reached the end of this interview. Do you have any final message for the people following our website?

I do, and it is about this interview. You cannot imagine what pleasure I take in seeing that the Austrian analysis of the economy is finally gaining ground, and that you have asked the right questions. I'm always keen to speak to people, who don't accept the general mainstream theories as the only truth. The fact that people are interested to listen about the "Tragedy of the Euro" and want to hear more about Gold and Silver, shows that they have kept some great qualities; curiosity and the ability and willingness to think independently. Today, this is something rare to find. For most people it has become more convenient to repeat what the majority is telling them without making the effort to think freely, and to question the actual development.

I am very much looking forward to the conference itself. When I saw the subject and line-up I knew that the philosophy was right, and that the speakers would be interesting. For instance, it has been quite a while since I have seen Philipp (Dr. Bagus). I know him very well. He is really top gear when it comes to the euro. When in October of last year he was asked by the European Parliament to deliver a talk on the ECB, I was very happy. Not only for him personally, but also because the Austrian analysis makes sense to more and more people, even politicians. If Mises would still be alive, what would he think about our times? These are very exciting times. I therefore cannot wait to exchange views with Philipp.

How nice.

Yes. The fun part about this job is that you meet so many interesting people. People with a critical point of view. Take you guys for instance. Do you really think that organizing a conference with that title "The Tragedy of the Euro" is common? But nevertheless, you have a vision and you go for it. That is admirable. It will pay off in the future. And the conference will hit the bull's eye, I am sure.

Don't make us blush. You pay the coffee.

(Laughs.) Agreed! You know, investing is not just about money. It is about value. And where people are looking for value, that is where I feel comfortable.

Likewise. Thank you for this interview!

You are welcome!

Courtesy of Claudio Grass and Brecht Arnaert

Author's comment: For further information, or to enroll in the program, please call: (727) 564-9416.

Final Word

"The best form of financial privacy at the moment is physical gold, at least until a better option for digital currency hits the market. Gold may not be useful for day-to-day transactions, but as a store of value tucked away in an anonymous offshore facility, there is no better way of maintaining financial privacy."

—Simon Black, senior editor, SovereignMan.com (February 27, 2012)

THE COMING BANKING HOLIDAY

Our comment: I thoroughly endorse keeping your silver coins in the US and your gold bullion (coins or small bars) in Switzerland. In 2006, we opened an account with Credit Suisse Bank, purchasing as much gold and silver as we could then afford. In 2008, when the liquidity crisis hit, I called Credit Suisse and asked, "What would happen to our precious metals account if your bank went under?" The answer was, unfortunately, that the bank covers each account for $30,000 max. It was at that time that I decided to transfer my bullion holdings to a depository, and out of a bank.

Recently, I heard of a more substantial, less expensive Suisse depository, one that ICA, a respectable bullion dealer out of Durango, Colorado, recommended. I did my due diligence and was so impressed that I asked to join their "partnership" program. I'm happy to say that they also gave my small company the once-over and, after consideration, welcomed us.

Our action: We are in the process of transferring our gold bullion to Global Gold. We have moved our silver bullion to the Auckland Mint. In theory, you want to use silver as barter, during an emergency, and gold as a store of value. During a crisis, a pre-1965 dime would more than buy a loaf of bread. Using a gold Maple Leaf would pose a "change" problem. I am in the process now of educating all my clients about this logic: Keep your silver near you and your gold out of the country (lest it be confiscated). Historically, governments never confiscate silver, but frequently do gold.

CHAPTER SEVEN

"Reporting"

"Americans are motivated by money, not ideals. Washington is the home of despicable trickery at elections, underhanded tamperings with public officers, and cowardly attacks upon opponents, with scurrilous newspapers for shields and hired pens for daggers. I am disappointed. This is not the republic of my imagination."

—Charles Dickens (1842)

THE COMING BANKING HOLIDAY

*U*p until recently, reporting one's investments overseas was quite simple, and took just a few minutes and a first-class stamp. There was just one, one page form called the "FBAR" that needed to be filled out and sent to the US Treasury Department. As countries become desperate for tax money, as is the case now with America, they want to know where their citizens' money is stashed. Why are they now suddenly increasing our reporting obligations? Some say that in the near future, we can expect a "world tax," but let's just stay with what we know now.

As of April 2012, US tax filers with overseas accounts have to file at least one form (TD F-90-22.1) and, in many cases, a new form (TDF 8938). The first is commonly referred to as the FBAR, and the new one is entitled "Statement of Specified Foreign Assets."

The new form is not a Treasury Department form. It is a joint form of the IRS and the Treasury Department, and the form requests information on all of your foreign assets, not just foreign bank accounts.

In November, 2011, the IRS issued "Instructions for Form 8938." After quietly releasing a draft version of the new form, titled "Statement of Specified Foreign Financial Assets," they have provided instructions that now leave little doubt: US persons will be required to report all worldwide assets subject to exceptions and applicable threshold amounts.

In December 2011, the US Department of Treasury issued temporary regulations with respect to the Shadow FBAR.

The requirement to Form 8938 applies for taxable years beginning after March 18, 2010, which for most people will be their 2011 tax returns filed during 2012. The Department of Treasury also released proposed regulations applicable to certain domestic entities formed for the purpose of holding specified foreign financial assets.

For more detailed information and guidance, I recommend you download the Alert issued by Baker & McKenzie Zurich on January 11, 2012. It discusses the temporary regulations in Q&A format.

In conclusion, many US taxpayers with offshore assets will need to file two separate disclosure forms in 2012. The Shadow FBAR is required to be filed by April 15, in addition to the TDF 90-22.1 (US Treasury) to be filed by June 30. This includes bank accounts, pensions, stocks, annuities, and possibly land or real estate.

Many individual US taxpayers with offshore assets will have to file two separate disclosure forms with Uncle Sam in 2012 or risk draconian penalties. Here's how the two forms compare, according to the American Institute of CPAs.

Where to Disclose? Form 8938 and/or FBAR? (2011 Filings)

The following table helps one identify which foreign financial assets and accounts must be disclosed for 2011 on:

1. Form 8938, Statement of Specified Foreign Financial Assets;
2. Form TD F 90-22.1, Report of Foreign Bank and Financial Accounts (commonly referred to as FBAR); or,
3. both.

The table is based on information and guidance available as of January 19, 2012.

	ON FORM 8938	ON FORM TD F 90-22.1 (FBAR)
	(Required by Title 26—Internal Revenue Code)	(Required by Title 31—Bank Secrecy Act)
Where and when to file?	Filed with Form 1040 (by April 15th, or extended due date) to IRS	Received by FinCEN (a separate agency under the Department of the Treasury) no later than June 30th
Who must file?	Individuals	Individuals, estates, trusts, US business entities of all types, including disregarded entities
Minimum filing threshold	$50,000*	$10,000
Penalty for not filing	Civil: Up to $10,000 for each 30 days of non-filing, plus others; criminal penalties may also apply	Civil: Up to the greater of $100,000 or 50% of account balance in year of violation, plus others; criminal penalties may also apply
Examples of types of financial accounts and assets to be disclosed:		
Financial accounts *owned* by the individual and maintained at a foreign financial institution, including deposit accounts and mutual funds	Yes	Yes
Financial accounts maintained at a foreign financial institution over which the individual has *signature authority or control*, but no financial interest	No	Yes

7: "REPORTING"

Foreign retirement accounts, such as a pension or IRA equivalent	Yes	Yes, for some
Direct ownership of stock in a foreign corporation (not held in an account maintained by a financial institution)	Yes	No
Foreign partnership interests, such as foreign hedge funds and foreign private equity funds	Yes	No*
Foreign-issued life insurance products with a cash value	Yes	Yes
Foreign-issued annuity contracts	Yes	Yes
Interests in foreign financial assets with joint ownership	Yes, each joint owner must report separately	Yes, each joint owner must report separately
Undeveloped land—direct interest; indirect interest	Unclear	No
Real estate	Unclear	No
Personal property such as art, jewelry or car	No	No
Gold and other precious metals—bullion, certificates, ETF	Yes	Yes
Interests in foreign financial assets through constructive ownership situations:		
Reportable assets and accounts of a disregarded entity	Yes	Yes
Reportable assets and accounts of a foreign corporation or foreign partnership	Partly No	Yes, if own more than 50% of the entity

93

*The threshold applies to the aggregate value of all affected assets, as of December 31, 2011. It ranges from $50,000 for a single tax payer living in the US, to $400,000 for couples filing jointly, who live abroad. There are higher thresholds for intra-year asset values.

Courtesy of The American Institute of CPAs

7: "REPORTING"

Our comment: The reporting requirements for Americans are simple, and take but a few minutes to complete and send in. It is highly recommended that Americans having savings, investments, and possibly gold submit the required forms on a timely basis. Why are the Treasury and IRS monitoring their citizens so closely? While no one really knows, the theory is, in the future, a "world wealth tax" would be instituted. Interesting!

Our action: We are complying and are on the lookout for any new requirements. As mentioned, we will post any new regulatory forms on the blog as soon as we hear of them.

CHAPTER EIGHT

Opening an Offshore Trust

"Freedom is never more than one generation away from extinction. We didn't pass it to our children in the bloodstream. It must be fought for, protected, and handed on for them to do the same."

—Ronald Reagan

Foreign Trust: Offshore Asset Protection

Setting up a foreign trust is a good asset protection strategy that will add a strong layer of protection between your assets and any third party trying to get to your wealth. Its main difference, compared with a conventional trust, is that the foreign trust is often established in offshore jurisdictions, which will offer additional benefits and protection.

Why Establish a Trust?

If you are storing all of your assets in your home country, any bureaucrat can freeze your assets with the click of a mouse. Your wealth is at risk no matter how honest and law-abiding you are as a citizen. Having an offshore trust overseas is very much like storing all of your assets in a safely locked vault that is not owned by you. If someone goes after your assets and you

8: OPENING AN OFFSHORE TRUST

have correctly set up a trust, it doesn't matter if they try breaking down the vault door, because legally the assets inside don't belong to you anymore.

Establishing an offshore trust in the right jurisdiction is a great way to put some legal distance between you and your assets, providing an extra layer of protection. By holding assets in foreign accounts through a foreign trust, you're building a brick wall around your wealth.

Setting Up a Trust

Establishing a foreign trust can be very complicated and expensive if you don't know what you're doing. But you should not be scared away by the paperwork involved. This is a big step towards building your independence and resilience. Any paperwork is worth the additional protection you'll get from having your own trust. To set up a trust, you need capital. And while it's fully possible to start your trust with as little as $5000 the yearly costs are prohibitive with such a small amount. So if you don't have a fair amount of capital already, truth to be told a trust may not be for you.

A point worth mentioning is that setting up an offshore trust is not about hiding your money from the tax man. It is about diversifying your sovereign risk, i.e. not betting all your money on one horse—your home country.

The first and most important step for establishing a foreign trust is to choose a jurisdiction. You'll often find many trust companies based in Panama, Seychelles, Switzerland, and the Cayman Islands. Which one to choose? That depends.

IRS Form 3520: Don't Forget!

If you intend to create an offshore trust as a US citizen it's very important that you get familiar with IRS *Form 3520*, which is required annually to "Report Transactions with Foreign Trusts and Receipt of Certain Foreign Gifts."

Who Must File Form 3520?

If you're a US Citizen and fulfill one of the below circumstances you need to file Form 3520:

- Create or transfer money or property to a foreign trust
- Receive (directly or indirectly) any distributions from a foreign trust
- Receive certain gifts or bequests from foreign entities

Form 3520 Instructions have more detailed information about who must file a Form 3520; when and where to file, and possible penalties for late or incomplete filing.

More About Foreign Trusts

If you don't want to end up in jail with heavy fines, it's very important that you follow all reporting requirements of the IRS.

- *Foreign Trust Reporting Requirements*

It used to be illegal for the government to spy on citizens, but not anymore. You can end up on a "hot watch"-list where upon they can track your phone calls, emails, credit card purchases, etc. in real time.

8: OPENING AN OFFSHORE TRUST

- *Are they spying on you?*

Simon answers the question: Can the US government still freeze your bank accounts even though they are offshore?

- *Offshore Banking Q&A*

Need help with setting up a foreign trust?

To learn more about establishing a foreign trust and protecting your hard earned wealth and privacy, visit www.SovereignMan.com/Foreign-Trust and sign up for their free newsletter *Sovereign Man: Notes from the Field.*

Courtesy of Simon Black, Sovereign Man

Our comment: If your estate is large, or if you are in a profession that benefits from having a trust, then you should do it. Most of our clients here in NZ do not have a trust at the present time.

Our action: We do not have a trust at this time, and we recommend trusts to our clients based on a "need to have" basis.

CHAPTER NINE

Getting Yourself Out of Dodge

"Nothing is particularly hard if you divide it into small jobs."

—Henry Ford

THE COMING BANKING HOLIDAY

The question Monica and I get asked most frequently is this: When do you think it's going to hit the fan? Our answer: We're not waiting to find out! America—and the world, for that matter—is changing rapidly, and we recommend that each reader do his or her own homework, and make a decision accordingly. We had no intention of relocating permanently to NZ, but once we got here we were hooked. America is still our home, and always will be!

Who else better to go to, to learn more about this topic, but Doug Casey? Here is a recent interview.

Doug Casey on "Getting Out of Dodge," interviewed by Louis James, Editor, International Speculator

L: Doug, a lot of readers have been asking for guidance on how to know when it's time to exit center stage and hunker down in some safe place. Few people want to hide from the world in a cabin in the woods while life goes on in the mainstream, but nobody wants to get caught once the gates clang shut on the police state the US is becoming. How do you know when it's time to go?

Doug: Well, the first thing to keep in mind is that it's better to be a year too early than a minute too late. David Galland recently read *They Thought They Were Free: The Germans, 1933–45,* by Milton Mayer. He quoted a passage in his column of last Friday. It goes a long way in explaining why Americans appear to be such whipped dogs today. They're no different from the Germans of recent memory. For those who missed it, let me quote it:

> "You see," my colleague went on, "one doesn't see exactly where or how to move. Believe me, this is true. Each act, each occasion, is worse than the last, but only a little worse.

9: GETTING YOURSELF OUT OF DODGE

You wait for the next and the next. You wait for one great shocking occasion, thinking that others, when such a shock comes, will join with you in resisting somehow. You don't want to act, or even talk, alone; you don't want to 'go out of your way to make trouble.'... In the university community, in your own community, you speak privately to your colleagues, some of whom certainly feel as you do; but what do they say? They say, 'It's not so bad' or 'You're seeing things' or 'You're an alarmist.'

"These are the beginnings, yes; but how do you know for sure when you don't know the end, and how do you know, or even surmise, the end? On the one hand, your enemies, the law, the regime, the Party, intimidate you. On the other, your colleagues pooh-pooh you as pessimistic or even neurotic... the one great shocking occasion, when tens or hundreds or thousands will join with you, never comes. That's the difficulty. If the last and worst act of the whole regime had come immediately after the first and smallest, thousands, yes, millions would have been sufficiently shocked... But of course this isn't the way it happens. In between come all the hundreds of little steps, some of them imperceptible, each of them preparing you not to be shocked by the next. Step C is not so much worse than Step B, and, if you did not make a stand at Step B, why should you at Step C?"

The fact is that the US has been on a slippery slope for decades, and it's about to go over a cliff. However, our standard of living, while declining, is still very high, both relatively and absolutely. But an American can enjoy a much higher standard of living abroad.

On the other hand, if I were some poor guy in a poverty-wracked country with few opportunities, I'd want to go where the action

105

THE COMING BANKING HOLIDAY

is, where the money is, now. Today, that means trying to get into the United States. The US is headed the wrong direction, but it's still a land of opportunity and a whole lot better than some flea-bitten village in Niger.

L: By the time things get worse than some Third-World dictatorship in the US, such a person could have remitted a whole lot of cash back home.

Doug: And you'd have a whole lot of experiences that would give you a competitive edge back where you came from, or in the next place you go to. The one-eyed man is king in the valley of the blind. People have to lose that backward, peasant mentality that ties them to the land of their birth. Sad to say, although the average American has somewhat more knowledge of the world—mainly due to television—his psychology is just as constrained as that of some serf from central Asia or some primitive village in Africa. It's all a matter of psychology.

But if you're not poor, you want to go someplace that is safe, nice—whatever that means to you—and with a lower cost of living. As most readers know, for me that's *Cafayate, Argentina,* but one size does not fit all. It needs to be a place you actually enjoy spending some time, with people whose company you enjoy.

L: Fair enough. But our readers want to know if your guru-sense is tingling yet, or how close you think we are to it being too late to leave—or at least too late to leave with any meaningful assets.

Doug: I'm a trend observer. This is one of the advantages of studying history, because it shows you that things like this rarely happen overnight. They are usually the result of trends that build over years and years, sometimes over generations. In the case of the US, I think the trend has been downhill, in many ways, for many years. Pick a time. You could make an argument, from

9: GETTING YOURSELF OUT OF DODGE

a moral point of view, that things started heading downhill at the time of the *Spanish-American War*. That was when a previously peaceful and open country first started conquering overseas lands and staking colonies. America was still in the ascent towards its peak economically, but the seeds of its own demise were already sewn, and a libertarian watching the scene might have concluded that it was time to get out of Dodge.

L: [Laughs] That would have been a bit early....

Doug: [Chuckles] Yes, that would have been way too soon. As Adam Smith observed, there's a lot of ruin in a country.

L: On the other paw, it would have gotten you out before the War between the States, a disaster well worth avoiding.

Doug: No, the Spanish-American War was in 1898.

L: Oops! Sorry, I was thinking of what Americans call the *Mexican-American War,* but which Mexicans call the "American Invasion"—

Doug: [Laughs]

L: I'm not joking. That's what they called it in the history books I was given in Mexican schools when I lived there in the '70s. It has long seemed to me that that was an ominous turn for the worse for the US and a clear example of conquering a weaker neighbor purely for pillage—not just Texas, but everything from there all the way to California.

Doug: That's right. Davey Crockett and the boys, we love them, but in many ways they were the equivalent of today's Mexicans who want to recolonize the southwest and turn it back into part of Mexico, in what they call the Reconquista.

L: Indeed, but this is ancient history to most US taxpayers today—I'm reminded that it's not correct in many cases to call them Americans.

Doug: Yes, just as it was a misnomer to call the people who lived in the Roman Empire after Diocletian Romans—because Roman citizens were once free men. After about 300 AD most of them were bound to the land or their occupations as serfs. But the slide for Rome started at least 120 years earlier, after the death of Marcus Aurelius. Politically, the decline started with the accession of Julius Caesar 240 years before that. So, when did the slide—politically, economically, and socially—really start for the US? When were there no more trends going up?

L: FDR? The *New Deal* was really a moral, economic, and political turning point.

Doug: You could make that argument, but the US still grew economically, despite the roadblocks FDR threw in its path. US military power and global prestige continued growing from that point, although, paradoxically, the accelerating growth of the US military was directly responsible for the decline of the US economically and in terms of personal freedom. One reason for the ascendancy of the US after World War II was that we were the only major country in the world not physically devastated by the war.

L: Ah. Right.

Doug: So it seems to me that the peak of American civilization was in the 1960s. As for evidence, well, I like to put my finger on the *1959 Cadillac*. Those twin bullet taillights, the opulence of it.... In terms of then-current technology, things couldn't get much better.

9: GETTING YOURSELF OUT OF DODGE

L: "Opulence. I has it."

Doug: [Laughs—a real belly laugh] That's my favorite *TV commercial!* Anyway, that was the peak, in my mind. Though things continued getting better for a while, the US started to live out of capital.

L: Had to pay for guns and butter.

Doug: That's right. The Johnson administration's so-called Great Society created vast new federal bureaucracies that promised Americans free food, shelter, medical care, education, and what-have-you. Americans became true wards of the state. But the real, final nail in the coffin for America was in 1971 –

L: Nixon taking the US off the gold standard.

Doug: Nixon taking the US off the gold standard—*open devaluation of the dollar*, combined with wage and price controls for some months. And that was not long after the so-called Bank Secrecy Act, which abolished bank secrecy, and required the reporting of all foreign financial accounts. Nixon was, in many ways, even more of a disaster than Johnson. Republicans are usually worse than Democrats when it comes to freedom, partly because they like to couch their depredations in the rhetoric of defending the free market. While everyone understands that Democrats are socialists just under the surface, Republicans actually give capitalism a bad name. Baby Bush is a perfect, recent example.

L: But don't you worry your pretty little head about devaluation—it's just a "bugaboo"—and as long as you're not one of those unpatriotic people wanting to buy imports or vacation abroad, your dollar will be worth just as much tomorrow as it is today. The scary thing is that the Belarusian dictator Lukashenko said almost the same thing when the *Belarusian ruble lost two thirds of its forex value* earlier this year, asking his countrymen why they need to go on vacation in Germany or buy German cars..

Doug: You see why I like to study history? It doesn't repeat, but it sure does rhyme....

L: With a vengeance.

Doug: So, anyway, since 1971, some things have improved largely due to technological advances, but the America That Was has been fading into the past. It was a decisive turning point. You can see that in the accelerated proliferation of undeclared wars we've had since then. I don't just mean the penny-ante invasions of Granada and Panama—the US has always lorded it over Caribbean and Central American banana republics; those are just sport wars. But Iraq and Afghanistan are alien cultures on the other side of the world—apart from never posing any threat to the US. Now it looks like Iran and Pakistan are on the dance card, and they're big game. The War Against Islam has started in earnest, and it's going to end badly for the US. I explained all this at great length in the white paper, Learn to Make Terror Your Friend, that I wrote for *The Casey Report* last month.

Domestically, saying that the US is turning into a police state when you started this conversation was quite accurate. You can see more and more videos spreading over the Internet, not just of police brutality, but demonstrating the militarization and federalization of police, who are being inculcated with both disdain for and paranoia about ordinary citizens.

In the old days, if you were stopped for speeding, the peace [*sic*] officer was polite—you could get out of your car, meet the cop on neutral ground, and chat with him. You didn't have a serious problem unless you were obviously drunk or combative. Now,

9: GETTING YOURSELF OUT OF DODGE

you don't dare make a move. You better keep your hands in plain sight on the steering wheel and be ready for a Breathalyzer test without probable cause. The law enforcement officer will stand behind you with his hand on his gun. And you're the one who'd better be polite.

L: There has been a polar reversal. The cops used to address citizens as "sir" or "ma'am." Now, the correct response in a traffic stop is: "Yes, sir! I would love to inspect the bottom of your boot, sir!"

Doug: [Laughs] That's right. My friend Marc Victor gives out magnetized business cards. People ask, "Why?" He answers that it's so clients can put them on the bottom of their cars or refrigerators, so they can see it when the cops throw them to the ground.

L: Marc's a good man. There's a handy video on *Marc's website,* offering advice on what to do if you're pulled over by the police in a traffic stop.

Doug: A good public service announcement. At any rate, I think there's no question that the US has turned the corner on every basis: politically, socially, morally, and now, economically....

L: Okay, but, Doug, you said that in 1979 too. The question is, how do we know when the door is going to close?

Doug: [Laughs.] Well, sometimes I feel a little like the boy who cried wolf. But Roman writers like Tacitus and Sallust saw where Rome was going before it got completely out of control. Should they have said nothing, for fear of being too early? Here in the US, it should have gone over the edge back in the 1980s, but we got lucky. There was still a lot of forward momentum, which can last for decades when you're speaking of civilizations. There was the computer productivity boom. The Soviet

Union collapsed, China liberalized, and Communism was discredited everywhere except on US college campuses. The end of the Cold War opened up vast areas of the world to the global market. And most surprising of all, Volker tightened up the money supply and interest rates went high, causing people to save money and stop borrowing to consume.

L: That's not happening this time.

Doug: No. We got lucky back then. Since the '90s we've had a long and totally phony, debt-driven boom that's now come to an end. I feel very confident that there's no way out this time. There are huge distortions and misallocations of capital that have been cranked into the system for two decades. And not just in the US this time, but in Europe, China, Japan, and elsewhere.

The US is very clearly on the decline. The fact that in spite of bankrupting military expenditures to no gain for the American people, those in power are talking overtly and aggressively about attacking more countries—Iran and Pakistan in particular—is extremely grave. The fact that they attacked Libya—which, incidentally, is going to turn into a total disaster, a civil war that will last for years—shows it's not stopping. Sure, Obama brought troops home from Iraq—another disaster that's going to remain a disaster for years to come—but at the same time he put a company of combat troops in Uganda, of all places and Marines in Australia, to provoke the Chinese.

Back home, I've read reports that people are being stopped for carrying gold coins out of the US, in Houston in particular. Now we have *authorization of the military to detain US citizens*, on US soil, with no trail, and indefinitely, on the verge of becoming law. And *Predator Drones have been used to hunt down farmers* on their own ranches.

9: GETTING YOURSELF OUT OF DODGE

I could go on and on. This is not like spotting early signs of decay in America's expansionist wars of the 19th century or things getting worse with FDR. Most people can't see it with all the noise and confusion, but we've reached the edge of the precipice.

L: Don't worry about exactly where the edge is, just assume it's there and take appropriate action?

Doug: Yes. It really is there. It's a clear and present danger. But most Americans are as oblivious as most Germans were in the '30s. In fact, most of them support what's going on, just as most Germans supported their government in the '30s and '40s.

L: So...don't worry about figuring out exactly when the gates will shut. Assume they are shutting now?

Doug: That's right. One should be actively and vigorously looking to expatriate assets, cash, and even one's self. A prudent person will always be diversified politically and internationally.

L: What about people who have jobs they can't continue doing from abroad and who need the income?

Doug: They should still prepare, as best they can, to be ready to go on a vacation when things get hot—a vacation from which they might not return for a long time. All that needs happen, with the hysteria that's building in the US, is for a major terrorist incident—real or imagined—to occur. Homeland Security will lock the country down. I hate to admit it, but I'm almost starting to credit the *stories about those FEMA camps.*

Look, I know it sounds extreme, and the comparison to pre-WWII Germany has been made many times, but it bears repeating. Germany was the most literate, civilized, and even mellow, in some ways, country in Europe. It was much admired all around the world—a nation of shopkeepers, small farmers, and

THE COMING BANKING HOLIDAY

scholars. But the whole character of the place started changing in 1933, and it just got worse and worse. By the end of 1939, if you weren't out, you were done.

L: [Pauses] Well, not a cheerful thought. Actions to take?

Doug: Things we've said before: Set up foreign bank accounts in places you like to travel, while you can. Set up vault arrangements for physical precious metals outside the US. Buy foreign real estate that you'd like to own, because it can't be forcibly repatriated. Offshore asset protection trusts are a good idea too. Become an *International Man*. Let me emphasize that US taxpayers should stay within all US laws, because the consequences of breaking them are unbelievably draconian.

Generally, one simply must internationalize one's assets. The biggest danger investors face, by far, is not market risk—huge as that will be—but political risk. The only way to insulate yourself from such risk is to diversify yourself politically and geographically.

L: Right then...words to the wise. Thanks for your insight.

Doug: You're welcome. Most won't, but I just hope readers listen.

[For more specific investment advice and big-picture observations from Doug—as well as insightful analyses from other Casey Research experts, including Chief Economist Bud Conrad—give *The Casey Report* a test drive.]

Courtesy of Doug Casey, Casey Research, and Louis James, International Speculator

9: GETTING YOURSELF OUT OF DODGE

Our comment: I met Doug Casey in Auckland in 2010, when he was kind enough to invite his newsletter subscribers to a seaside dinner (very generous fellow). I have tried to follow his investment philosophy ever since. As to whether you should relocate to a foreign country, I really don't think it necessary. However, what *is* necessary is for you to do your homework, and have your "run-to" country in mind, if the time ever comes to leave. For those interested in obtaining residency here in NZ, I will gladly answer all e-mails and advise on the formalities.

Our action: Needless to say, we are here in NZ. We arrived in March 2009.

CHAPTER TEN

A Simple Plan to Keep Your Assets Safe from an Out-of-Control Government

"In 2012 America will become a battlefield of the will of the people against the will of the government."

—Gerald Celente, founder, Trends Research Institute

By keeping all your assets in the country where you live, you commit, ahead of time, to ratify whatever policy your home government might adopt, no matter how objectionable, unreasonable, or pernicious that policy happens to be. If the next new mandate is "Register today to get a nail pounded into your head," you're already signed up.

Americans, by and large, run all their affairs within the confines of the US. The US economy is so large and so varied that it's easy to assume that everything you want to do with your wealth can be done without crossing any borders. And people in the US, like people anywhere, live with the habits and attitudes developed over generations. They're only human. In the case of Americans, those habits grew out of long experience with a government that was small and that generally practiced the rare virtue of following its own laws. In a happy exception to mankind's experience with rulers, there was little to fear from it.

Stay at home is still the norm for Americans, but it's a norm that is slowly fading. Every billion-dollar tick of the government debt clock, every expansion of the government's regulatory apparatus, every overreaching judicial decision made in the name of a compelling public need, every inversion of protection for citizens into license for the state, and every intellectually tortured discovery of a new meaning in the Constitution's 4,400 old words leaves a few thousand more people wondering how prudent it is to consign all their eggs to a single national basket. Encounters with high-handed IRS agents and eager TSA gropers do nothing to ease that concern. And for those who listen thoughtfully, the messages from our designated leaders and their would-be replacements only hurry the dawning sense of unease.

Specific worries include exposure to predatory lawsuits, especially claims that could draw extra go-power by association

10: A SIMPLE PLAN TO KEEP YOUR ASSETS SAFE...

with politically favored causes or legally favored groups; fear of where income tax rates might climb; the prospect of losing a family business in a regulatory battle or simply through estate tax; the fragility of financial institutions that have operated for forty years with the assurance that the Federal Reserve would rescue them from any folly; the possibility that a government desperate to protect the dollar from collapse might impose foreign exchange controls or capital controls; the memory and precedent of the forced gold sales of 1933; and the thought that a government floundering in deficits might start pilfering from IRAs and other pension plans.

But beyond those particular worries and perhaps more important than any of them is the sense that from here on, anything goes. The politicians will do whatever they find convenient, because there is no longer anything to stop them—not an electorate that is jealous of its freedoms and certainly not the Constitution, which is now just a playhouse for judicial imagin-eering. No one can know what's coming next from the government and the financial system it has fostered, but for many of us there is an awful suspicion that we are not going to like it.

Most Americans still have yet to stick a single financial toe across the border, but more and more are considering it. Many, perhaps millions of toes are now twitching at the thought. Their owners want to end their absolute dependence on what happens in the US. They want to prepare for whatever is coming down the road, even though they don't know what it will be. They want to be as ready as possible, even though their worries can only guess at what's ahead.

Because internationalizing your financial life means dealing with the unfamiliar, the project can seem more complex than it really is, so it's best to start with the simplest measures, even if by themselves they don't give you all the safety you're looking for. Even from a simple beginning, what you learn with each step will make the next step easier to plan. Start with the first rung on the ladder of internationalization. Then climb, at your own speed, to reach the right level of protection.

Rung 1: Coins in Your Pocket

Gold coins that you've stored personally give you something whose value doesn't depend on the health of the US economy, doesn't depend on any financial institution in the US and doesn't depend on any US government policy. Gold coins are portable and hold their value no matter where in the world you might take them. They're internationalization in a wafer. Safety cookies.

It's best to buy the coins for cash, for maximum privacy. And there is a good reason to favor one-tenth-ounce gold Eagles. Gold coins mean readiness for troubled times; if you ever need to dispose of the gold in an informal market, it will be easier to do so with small-denomination coins that are widely recognizable and whose value matches the scale on which large numbers of people normally trade.

The premium on one-tenth-ounce coins (the price compared with the value of the gold content) is higher than on the larger coins—usually about 15% for the small coins vs. 5% for one-ounce Eagles. But the premium isn't a dead cost, like a commission or bid-ask spread. The premium is a second investment; it's what you pay for the packaging, and you can expect to recover it when you sell or trade. And in the circumstances when you would have the strongest reasons for thanking yourself for having bought some gold, the premium you paid will look like a bargain.

10: A SIMPLE PLAN TO KEEP YOUR ASSETS SAFE...

Rung 2: A Foreign Bank Account

On its own initiative, the IRS can freeze any bank account in the US without warning. The action might arise from mistaken identity, from an erroneous filing by some other taxpayer, from your failure to respond to an IRS notice in time or even from a postal error. And that's what can happen without malice. Other government agencies have similar powers to act on their own, without giving you an opportunity to object in court. And any one of them might act against you for any of their specialized reasons—perhaps because someone resents your inattention to the needs of the migratory birds that visit your property or perhaps because someone thinks it would be fun to point to you as a terrorist, drug smuggler, arms dealer or child-porn merchant.

In principle, there are legal avenues for undoing a freeze or a seizure. But you'd need a lawyer, and being suddenly penniless could get in the way of hiring one.

A foreign bank account protects you from being trapped in such a nightmare. The US government can get to your foreign bank account eventually, because it can get to you. But a lightning seizure is very unlikely, because it would require a foreign government to override its own legal processes, which it generally wouldn't be willing to do except in a grave emergency. So if your liquid assets at home were frozen, you would have cash outside the US to fund the legal cost of untangling the problem.

A foreign bank account is also a way to step back from the uncertainties of the US dollar, since the account could be denominated in another currency.

The US government has seen to it that Americans are no longer welcome customers at foreign banks. So forget about opening a Swiss bank account in your own name. However, if you apply in person (not by mail), you still can open a bank account in

Canada. Be prepared to show your passport and to give the bank an original utility bill that confirms your place of residence.

Rung 3: Gold Abroad

The forced gold sales of 1933 were the work of an executive order signed by President Roosevelt. The purported legal basis for the order was the Trading With the Enemy Act, a legislative artifact of World War I. I have yet to find an explanation of how the authority for an order requiring Americans to sell their gold to the government at the government's official price of $20 per ounce could be found in the Trading With the Enemy Act, but the fact that the enemy in question had gone out of business 15 years earlier didn't seem to interfere with the legal logic.

The forced sale was a prelude to an increase in the official gold price to $35. The government's reason for wanting that price rise was to gain leeway for a substantial, though limited, inflation of the dollar while keeping the dollar on the international gold standard. The forced sale was a way for the government, which operated in a political environment that still disfavored deficit spending, to capture the profit from the price rise. That profit would be a kitty for more spending without more borrowing.

Today there is no gold standard for the government to stay on. And deficit spending isn't something politicians especially want to avoid; they've promoted it as a civic duty, to stimulate the economy. So the depression-era motives for a gold grab don't seem to apply. Yet you can't listen to a conversation between two gold investors without hearing the seizure topic coming up.

Are they just scaring each other? I don't believe so. There are two potential motives for the government to again treat gold differently from everything else.

If the dollar's slide in foreign exchange markets threatens to turn into a panic, the government might want to use gold sales to foreigners to mop up foreign-held dollars—in which case it might see a need to mop up the gold owned by its own citizens. That's bad enough, but a second motive is a good bit nastier. At a visceral level, people who have centered their lives on government just don't like gold. It's an affront to the government's authority to command and control and an insult to government's supposed aptitude for solving economic problems. So disrespectful! From their point of view, every ounce purchased by an American is another tomato hurled at the political class. And the purchasers still constitute a tiny minority of the voting population.

What could be more satisfying and convenient for the politicians than to kick sand in the face of gold investors for being such lousy citizens?

A new attack on gold ownership probably wouldn't be a point-for-point reenactment of 1933. There are many weapons for mugging gold investors. It could be a prohibition on gold ownership coupled with a prohibition on sales of gold to foreigners. The only one left to buy would be the government, and being the only bidder, it would be a very low bidder. It could be a commandeering of privately owned gold, with token compensation like the $15 per day paid for jury duty. It could be a super tax, say 90%, on gold profits, which would get the job done slowly... or quickly if it were accompanied by a mark-to-market rule. Or it could be something none of us has thought of yet.

Not only can't we know the shape of a future gold grab, we can't know whether or how the rules would touch foreign-held gold. Owners of gold stored outside the US would be a minority of a minority. Their gold wouldn't be the low-hanging fruit—it would be higher up in the tree and more trouble to get to. That's why, in a casino sense, gold overseas is a different bet and a better bet than gold at home.

Maybe it will turn out that storing gold overseas won't matter at all, in which case a little effort will have been wasted. And maybe it will turn out to matter a great deal.

Rung 4: A Swiss Annuity

A conventional annuity contract is a device for accumulating investment returns and eventually converting the value into a lifetime income. The investment return on an annuity from a US insurance company is tax deferred until it is paid out to you. If you buy an annuity from a foreign company, tax deferral is available only if the annuity's value is tied to the performance of a pool of investments (a variable annuity).

Swiss annuities have long held a special place in personal financial planning. Such an annuity is denominated in Swiss francs, i.e., it's francs, not dollars, that are owed to you. The Swiss insurance industry has a perfect record; policyholders have never been hurt by a default. And a Swiss annuity comes with an element of protection from would-be lawsuit creditors.

The Swiss franc is, like every other modern-day currency, just a piece of paper. It's not redeemable for anything, not even a piece of chocolate. But the Swiss National Bank has a remarkable record of restraint in issuing new francs, which means that the franc's prospects for holding its value have long been rated better than for any other currency.

I believe that is still the case, despite the Swiss National Bank's current policy of suppressing any further increase in the price of the franc. In September, in order to save export industries from being crushed by the franc's rapid appreciation against other currencies, the Swiss National Bank announced that it would purchase euros without limit to enforce a minimum exchange rate of 1.2 francs per euro—which implies printing enough francs to pay for those euros. By itself, it is an inflationary move, but it's not a suicide pact with the European Central Bank (the issuing authority for euros). If the ECB turns to a policy of rapid inflation, I would expect the Swiss National Bank at some point to decouple the franc from the euro and let the franc's price rise. So owning some Swiss francs, whether directly or through an annuity, is still a good step toward internationalizing your financial life.

Under Swiss law, an annuity is protected from the owner's creditors if the beneficiaries consist of family members or if the owner has made a beneficiary designation that is irrevocable. For an owner in the US, that protection is not an impenetrable barrier to the winner of a lawsuit, but it is a barrier, and it makes the annuity a less-than-ideal prize for an attacker.

Earnings that are accumulating in a Swiss annuity are not eligible for tax deferral for a US taxpayer. The advantages are currency protection, the reliability of Swiss insurance companies and a measure of asset protection.

Rung 5: Foreign Real Estate

Owning real estate in another country gives you a suite of protections that distinguishes it from other steps toward internationalization.

First, the property's value will depend on economic conditions in the country you've chosen, not on what happens in the US. If the economy of the foreign country grows and prospers, there is likely to be a spillover effect on the market value of your house, apartment, farm or patch of land—regardless of what is going on in the US.

Second, a foreign real estate investment would be hard to digest for any future capital controls imposed by the US. New rules could compel you to repatriate the cash you have in a foreign bank; rules forcing you to liquidate your foreign real estate and bring the money home would be another matter. Selling real estate isn't quick or easy. How does the government compel an unwilling citizen to do what an eager seller often finds difficult to accomplish?

Third, as a potential prize for a lawsuit attacker, foreign real estate is a stinker. Even if he wins a judgment against you, foreclosing on your foreign property would be difficult to impossible, since it would require the cooperation of the courts in the foreign country, about whose rules and procedures the attacker's attorney probably knows nothing. But he does know that even if he persuades a court in the US to order you to sell the property, the inherent illiquidity of real estate would give you plenty of opportunities for foot-dragging.

Where to buy? The whole world is open to you... which can be a problem. So many possibilities and no obvious place to start. One approach is to think about where you've been that you'd like to visit again or about some place you've long wanted to see. Plan to spend a few weeks there. Minimize your hotel hours, to maximize your exposure to the rest of the locale. Try to meet Americans, perhaps expatriates, who know their way around the place and who can point you toward a real estate broker who won't try to treat you as an out-of-town sucker.

Buying foreign real estate isn't for everyone. It requires a big investment in time and effort, but it could repay you with an asset that is low on the list of things anyone might try to take from you.

10: A SIMPLE PLAN TO KEEP YOUR ASSETS SAFE...

Rung 6: A Foreign LLC for Investments

A limited liability company organized under the laws of a foreign country is easy to set up and not too expensive. To bring the company into existence, you (or a service you hire) would file a simple form with a government office in the country you've chosen and pay a small fee. Then you as the LLC's Manager and you as the LLC's owner would enter into an agreement (the "operating agreement") that would be the company's governing instrument.

As the LLC's Manager, you would open a non-US bank account or brokerage account in the name of the LLC and transfer your personal cash and investments to that account. Again as Manager, you would make all the investment decisions.

For a US person, a foreign LLC can be a powerful door opener. It is welcome at many banks and brokerage firms where you personally would be turned away. This enables you to keep a wider range of assets outside the US, which puts more wealth beyond the reach of any arbitrary bureaucratic action. It also gives you investment choices that aren't available at home.

Access to foreign investments and overseas financial services is reason enough to consider using a foreign limited liability company. But it can do much more for you, although at the cost of some complexity.

Notice the fundamental difference between a foreign LLC and what is going on at the first four rungs of the ladder of internationalization. With the LLC, you no longer personally own the assets you are trying to protect; the company owns them. This makes the LLC a powerful device for reducing your family's expose to gift and estate taxes. And with the right provisions in the operating agreement, it can provide strong protection against loss to any malicious lawsuit.

If you are the sole owner of a foreign LLC intended for holding investments, you can and almost certainly should file an election for the LLC to be treated as a disregarded entity (indistinguishable from you for income tax purposes). If your spouse or anyone else is going to share in ownership of the LLC, the company can and should elect to be treated as a partnership for income tax purposes.

Rung 7: A Foreign LLC for Business

A business that operates outside the US does even more than a portfolio of foreign investments to give you the benefits of internationalization.

By its nature, a foreign business lives in a different environment than a business in the US. Economic troubles at home might not touch it. If it's a business that depends on your personal efforts, it's even less attractive as a lawsuit prize than foreign real estate. Being foreign, it would be outside the range of capital controls in the US. And many of the financial institutions that might turn away an investment-owning LLC because it is owned by an American will welcome an LLC that makes or sells goods or services.

If you already have a business in the US that has foreign customers or foreign suppliers, you may be able to relocate the business's non-US activities to a foreign LLC. Internet-based businesses are especially amenable to internationalization.

Locating your business in a low-tax or no-tax jurisdiction, if it is practical to do so, can reduce your overall tax burden. In many cases, a foreign LLC that operates a business should elect to be treated as a foreign corporation for US income tax purposes. That can allow the business to reinvest its earnings while it pays little in current taxes and you personally pay nothing.

10: A SIMPLE PLAN TO KEEP YOUR ASSETS SAFE...

Rung 8: An International Trust That You Establish

Establishing a trust outside the US is the strongest internationalization step you can take for yourself and your family. Doing so costs more than any other measure, but the costs needn't be prohibitive if your goal is to move $500,000 or more into the safest structure possible. What you achieve is a very high level of protection from aggressive lawsuits, from potential capital controls and from the possibility of a gold seizure. The trust also puts your wealth in a far better environment for income tax planning and for estate planning.

To serve the purposes of protection and tax savings, an international trust is irrevocable (you can't simply call the institution you've chosen as trustee and say you've changed your mind) and discretionary (meaning that the trustee has a responsibility to decide when to send a check to you or to any of the other beneficiaries you've included). Putting assets under the control of a trust company under such an arrangement is a big step. You're not going to do it unless you've done the homework needed to understand how and why you can count on the trustee to handle the assets in the way you intend.

Getting the protection and tax savings of an international trust doesn't require you to give up management control of the assets. The trust can be limited to owning just one thing—an LLC that you manage. The LLC owns all the investments, under your supervision as LLC Manager.

If you establish an international trust, it will be tied to you for income tax purposes. But at the end of your lifetime, it will completely disconnect from the US tax system. At that point, for the benefit of your survivors, it becomes...

Rung 9: An International Trust Someone Else Established

Being a beneficiary of an international trust established by someone other than a living US person is as good as it gets. It's not linked to you by any transfers you've made to it, and you don't have a determinable percentage interest in it (since it's a discretionary trust). So until you actually receive a distribution, there is nothing for you to report, nothing for you to pay tax on and nothing a potential lawsuit creditor can hope to take from you. And, having no living connection to the US, the trust is as far beyond the orbit of any conceivable US gold seizure or currency controls as the former planet Pluto.

One Toe over the Line

It's a long way from walking into the local coin shop and buying a few one-tenth-ounce gold Eagles to setting up a trust in a foreign country. But the distance isn't nearly as great as you might imagine, and it will get shorter both in fact and in apprehension with each step you take.

As you move up the ladder, you'll learn about the reporting requirements for US taxpayers. Rung 1 (gold coins in your pocket) entails no reporting, nor does Rung 8 until you actually receive a distribution. Rung 5 (foreign real estate) also is free of reporting requirements, at least for now. But under rules in effect now or soon to come, everything else covered in this article entails filing a form with the US government. The most reliable way to make sure that you stay within the rules, so that internationalization adds to your safety and not to your problems, is to let your accountant know what you are doing. Keep him informed, so that he can see to it that all the reporting requirements are satisfied.

Courtesy of Terry Coxon, Casey Research

10: A SIMPLE PLAN TO KEEP YOUR ASSETS SAFE...

Our comment: Terry's article is so comprehensive that it could be the book. He's got so many great points; I agree with all of them except the Suisse annuity and real estate. It is my opinion that, as you make your move to a new country, you stay as liquid as possible. While the Suisse annuity is quite liquid, and much better than the American annuities that I used to market when I was a broker, it is still an annuity. Real estate is not easy to sell, should it become necessary to exit the country quickly. Better to rent.

Our action: We did form a corporation here in NZ when we applied for our entrepreneurial work visa, but it wasn't an LLC. Rentals are reasonable in Auckland, and housing dear. Therefore we rented and, in all likelihood, will continue to rent. With gold rising on the average 20% a year, and housing prices falling about 13% a year, it makes sense to rent.

CHAPTER ELEVEN

Porter Stansberry's Stern Message

"Everyone loves an early inflation. The effects at the beginning of inflation are all good. There is steepened money expansion, rising government spending, increased government budget deficits, booming stock markets, and spectacular prosperity, all in the midst of temporary stable prices. Everyone benefits, and no one pays."

—Jens O. Parsson, *Dying of Money*

THE COMING BANKING HOLIDAY

*O**f all of Wall Street's forecasters, Porter Stansberry is considered foremost. In my line of work, I have to subscribe to numerous monthly newsletters, and Porter's ranks right up there.*

He warned investors to avoid Fannie and Freddie, Bear Stearns, Lehman Brothers, General Motors, and dozens of other companies that have since collapsed. He even helped subscribers find opportunities to profit from these moves by shorting stocks and buying put options. To my knowledge, no other research firm in the world matched his record of correctly predicting the catastrophe that occurred in 2008.

He now believes there is an even bigger crisis lurking—something that will shake the very foundation of America. He talks about a specific event that will take place in America's very near future, which could actually bring our country and our way of life to a grinding halt.

Here's his recent powerful, shocking letter to his subscribers, many of whom cancelled their subscription (those apparently in denial), but most agreed that it was time to face the truth.

This looming crisis is related to the financial crisis of 2008... but it is infinitely more dangerous, as I'll explain in this letter. As this problem comes to a head, I expect there to be riots in the streets...arrests on an unprecedented scale...and martial law, enforced by the US military.

Believe me, I don't make this prediction lightly and I have no interest in trying to scare you. I'm simply following my research to its logical conclusion. I did the same when I tracked Fannie and Freddie's accounting; the same with General Motors, Bear Stearns and the rest. And when I began giving this warning in 2006 no one took me very seriously...not at first. Back then, most mainstream commentators just ignored me.

11: PORTER STANSBERRY'S STERN MESSAGE

And when I presented my case and exposed the facts at economic conferences, they got angry. They couldn't refute my research...but they weren't ready to accept the enormity of its conclusions either.

That's why, before I go any further, I have to warn you.... What I am going to say is controversial. It will offend many people... Democrats, Republicans, and Tea Partiers, alike. In fact, I've already received dozens of pieces of hate mail. And...the ideas and solutions I'm going to present might seem somewhat radical to you at first...perhaps even "un-American." My guess is that, as you read this letter...you'll say: "There's no way this could really happen...not here." But just remember: No one believed me three years ago when I said the world's largest mortgage bankers Fannie Mae and Freddie Mac would soon go bankrupt.

And no one believed me when I said GM would soon be bankrupt as well...or that the same would happen to General Growth Properties (the biggest owner of mall property in America). But again, that's exactly what happened. And that brings us to today.

The same financial problems I've been tracking from bank to bank, from company to company for the last five years have now found their way into the US Treasury. I'll explain how this came to be. What it means is critically important to you and every American.... The next phase in this crisis will threaten our very way of life.

The savings of millions will be wiped out. This disaster will change your business and your work. It will dramatically affect your savings accounts, investments, and retirement. It will change everything about your normal way of life: where you vacation...where you send you kids or grandkids to school...how and where you shop...the way you protect your family and home.

I'll explain how I know these events are about to happen. You can decide for yourself if I'm full of hot air. *As for me, I'm more certain about this looming crisis than I've been about anything else in my life.* I know that debts don't just disappear. I know that bailouts have big consequences. And, unlike most of the pundits on TV, I know a lot about finance and accounting.

Of course, the most important part of this situation is not what is happening...but rather what you can do about it. In other words: Will you be prepared when the proverbial $@*% hits the fan? Don't worry, I'm not organizing a rally or demonstration. And I've turned down every request to run for political office. Instead, I want to show you exactly what I'm doing personally, to protect and even grow my own money, and how you can prepare as well.

You see, I can tell you with near 100% certainty that most Americans will not know what to do when commodity prices—things like milk, bread and gasoline—soar. They won't know what to do when banks close...and their credit cards stop working. Or when they're not allowed to buy gold or foreign currencies. Or when food stamps fail.... In short, our way of life in America is about to change—I promise you. In this letter I'll show you exactly what is happening. You can challenge every single one of my facts and you'll find that I'm right about each allegation I make. And then you can decide for yourself.

Will you act now to protect yourself and your family from the catastrophe that's brewing right now in Washington? I hope so. And that's why I wrote this letter. I'm going to walk you through exactly what I am doing personally, and what you can do as well. I can't promise you'll emerge from this crisis completely unharmed—but I can just about guarantee you'll be a lot better off than people who don't follow

11: PORTER STANSBERRY'S STERN MESSAGE

these simple steps. But I'm getting ahead of myself just a bit. Let me back up and show you in the simplest terms possible what is going on, why I am so concerned, and what I believe will happen in the next 12 months.... The Greatest Danger America Has Ever Faced? In short, I believe that we as Americans are about to see a major, major collapse in our national monetary system, and our normal way of life. Basically, for many years now, our government has been borrowing so much money (very often using short-term loans), that very soon, we will no longer be able to afford even the *interest* on these loans.

Again...I say these things as an expert in accounting and financial research.

You may not think things are THAT BAD in the US economy, but consider this simple fact from the National Inflation Association: Even if all US citizens were taxed 100% of their income... it would still not be enough to balance the Federal budget! We'd still have to borrow money, just to maintain the status quo. That's absolutely incredible, isn't it?

Yet I've never seen this fact reported anywhere else. Normally I study these kinds of numbers when I'm looking at a business to invest in or to recommend to my readers. But lately I've spent most of my time looking into our national balance sheet, because as the banking system collapsed in 2008, all of the bad debts were absorbed by the world's governments. For example, when Fannie Mae and Freddie Mac collapsed in the summer of 2008, the US government responded by simply guaranteeing all of their outstanding debt.

Since then these companies have recorded hundreds of billions of losses—all of which were passed along to the government. Yes, you can still get mortgages today. And yes, Freddie and Fannie are still in business. But costs associated with these programs

THE COMING BANKING HOLIDAY

are piling up at the US Treasury—and they are enormously expensive. These losses and trillions in other private obligations are now the responsibility of the US government. The problem is, even before this crisis, our government was deeply in debt. With each additional commitment we sink further and further into debt...closing in upon the moment that we can simply no longer afford even the interest payments on our obligations.

According to even my most conservative calculations (using numbers provided by the Congressional Budget Office) a debt default by the US government would be inevitable—were it not for one simple anomaly... the one thing that has saved the United States so far. I'm talking about our country's unique ability to simply print more money. You see, the US government has one very important weapon to use in this crisis: It is the only debtor in the world who can legally print US dollars. And the US dollar is what's known as "the world's reserve currency." The dollar forms the basis of the world's financial system. It is what banks around the world hold in reserve against their loans. That's a secret that most politicians don't understand. As things stand now, the US government can't go broke in any ordinary sense of the word because it can simply print dollars to pay for its bad debts. (It's been doing so since March of 2009). That might sound pretty good at first. Since we can always just print more money, what is there to worry about...?

Well, let me show you.... You see, as things stand today, America is the only country in the world that doesn't have to pay for its imports in a foreign currency. Let's say you're a German and you want to buy oil from Saudi Arabia. You can't just pay for your oil in German marks (or the new euro currency), because the oil is priced in dollars. So you have to buy dollars first, then buy your oil. And that means the value of the German currency is of great importance to the German government. To maintain the value of its currency Germans must produce at least as much as they consume from around the world, otherwise the value of its currency will begin to fall, causing prices to rise and its standard of living to decline.

But in America...? We can consume as much as we want without worrying about acquiring the money to pay for it, because our dollars are accepted everywhere around the word. In short, for decades now, we haven't had to produce anything or export anything to get all the dollars we needed to buy all the oil (and other goods) our country required. All we had to do was borrow the money. And boy did we. Take a look at this chart.

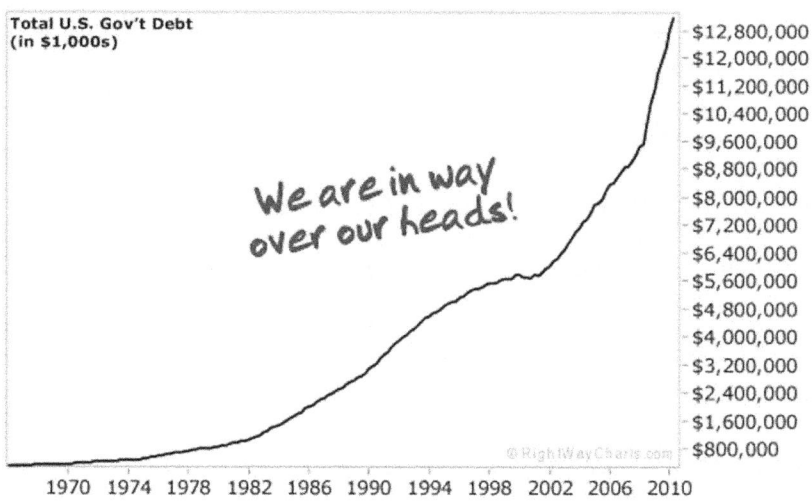

Even as late as the 1970s, America was the world's largest creditor. But by the mid-1980s we'd become a debtor to the world. And since the late 1990s we've been the world's LARGEST debtor. Today, our government owes more money to more people than anyone else in the world. And that was before the financial crisis! In short, with all of these bad debts piling up, we've had to begin repaying our debts by printing trillions of new dollars. The impact of this is only just now beginning to be felt. And once our creditors figure out what's happening, they're going to be very angry. I believe they will either completely stop accepting dollars in repayment... or greatly discount the value of these new dollars. I'm sure you think that sounds crazy, but as I'll show you, it is already happening.

And that will make our consumption-led way of life impossible to afford. Just think about the price of oil.... Access to cheap oil has been America's #1 gift of owning the world's reserve currency. This, along with several other government policies, has made gas cheaper in the US than almost anywhere else in the developed world. I know you may think gas prices have skyrocketed in recent years...but look at how much less we pay than other developed nations...

- United States: $2.72 a gallon on average
- Oslo, Norway: $7.41.........(172% higher)
- Berlin, Germany: $6.82....(151% higher)
- London: $6.60...................(143% higher)
- Rome, Italy: $6.40..............(135% higher)
- Paris, France: $6.04...........(122% higher)
- Tokyo, Japan: $5.40...........(98% higher)
- Toronto, Canada: $3.81......(40% higher)

According to the most recent study (March 2011) by Kiplinger's Personal Finance, we pay around $3.61 a gallon on average, here in the US. But in Canada, it's $5.56, the French pay a whopping $8.21, the Japanese pay $6.62, Australians pay $5.41, and the Chinese pay $4.54.

11: PORTER STANSBERRY'S STERN MESSAGE

And here's the thing...if oil is no longer priced in dollars, the price of oil for Americans will skyrocket immediately. It will change our lives, overnight.

Airline travel will get much more expensive. The cost to ship goods by truck to grocery stores around the country will get much more expensive. Farming itself will get a lot more costly... so will commuting to work...taking a taxi...just about everything we do will suddenly get much more expensive. And just remember: In order for prices to start skyrocketing, all that has to happen is that other countries start preferring payments in something besides US dollars.

The US dollar has been the world's currency for decades now... so most Americans don't have a clue about what the repercussions are of losing this status. You might think this could never happen...but it happens all the time when countries get too far in debt or when they consume too much or produce too little. In fact, the same thing happened to Great Britain in the 1970s. Most people don't know this, but British Sterling was the reserve currency for most of the world for nearly 200 years...for most of the 18th and 19th centuries.

It continued to play this role until after World War II, when America was forced to prop up Britain's economy with foreign aid—remember the famous Marshall Plan, when we gave billions to help European countries rebuild? Unfortunately though, Britain pursued a socialist national agenda. The government took over all of the major industries. Like Barack Obama, Britain's leaders wanted to "spread the wealth around." Pretty soon the country was flat broke. The final straw for Britain came in 1967, when things got so bad the Labour Party (the socialists) decided to "devalue" the British currency by 14%, overnight. They believed this would make it easier for people to afford their debts.

In reality, what it did was make anyone holding British sterling 14% poorer, overnight, and it made everything in Britain, much, much more expensive in the coming years. And for the country as a whole, it ushered in one of the worst decades in modern British history. Most Americans don't know about Britain's "Winter of Discontent" in the late 1970s, when the government put a freeze on wages. There were continuous strikes in nearly every sector...grave diggers, trash collectors...even hospital workers. Things got so bad at one point that many hospitals were reduced to accepting emergency patients only. In 1975, inflation in Britain skyrocketed 26.9%...in a single year!

The government also imposed what was known as the "Three Day Week" in 1974. In short, businesses were limited to using electricity for only three specified consecutive days' [sic] each week and they were prohibited from working longer hours on those days. Television companies were required to cease broadcasting at 10.30pm...to save electricity. The extreme problems in the economy led to Britain being nicknamed, "the sick man of Europe."

Just how bad were things, exactly? Well, listen to several Brits tell of their experiences. Their stories were collected recently by the BBC television channel...John Blackburn, from Wetherby said:

"I was a control engineer at Huddersfield Power Station at the time and part of my duty was to switch off the supply to various substations around the town, according to an official rota. On many an evening shift I would have to switch off the power to my own home before going back for a candle-lit supper!" Richard Evans, from London, recalls: "My mother had to cross a picket line to get into the maternity hospital (they told her she couldn't come in....). My Grandmother had to bring in food for her to eat, and clean towels and bedding."

11: PORTER STANSBERRY'S STERN MESSAGE

David Stoker, Guildford, said: "I lived in the North East near Newcastle and I vividly remember my grandmother and I walking from one shop to another in search of candles to buy. All were sold out. Innovatively, butchers placed string down cartons of drippings which we bought.... These worked although the smell and risk of fire made them less practical than candles."

Imagine...Britain was a global superpower for 150 years. But when they started intentionally devaluing their currency, things went straight down hill. Maybe you don't think something similar can happen here...but I'm telling you...it's already underway! In fact, the exchange value of the US dollar has plummeted in the past year. Look at this chart.

From June first of 2010 to June 1st of 2011, the US dollar has plunged 12%. That's a huge move in the currency world. In short, people are quickly losing faith in the US dollar. What happened to the British currency is now happening to the US dollar. Not only will the price of gas, oil, and other commodities skyrocket in America, almost EVERYTHING we consume will

THE COMING BANKING HOLIDAY

immediately get more expensive. All the clothing, furniture, and household goods we import from China.

All the food we get from Central and South America...all the electronics, televisions, computers, and cars we get from Asia and Europe.

In fact, it's happening, right now before our eyes: The price of gold is up 85% since the financial crisis. Oil prices have doubled. Soy beans are way up. Copper prices are up more than 170% since 2009. *Cotton prices are up 80%...in just the past few months, since July of this year!* In fact, it's happening right now before our eyes: The price of gold is up more than 100% since the financial crisis of 2009. See Kitco historical gold prices. IN [sic] the beginning of Nov. 2008, gold was trading for less than $740. Now it's over $1,500, so it's up more than 100%. As Wesley Card, the head of a clothing company that includes brands like Dockers and Anne Klein, recently said: "It's really a no-choice situation. Prices have to come up."

Of course, skyrocketing commodity prices are just the beginning. There are other disastrous consequences to the US dollar losing status as the world's currency.... For example, there would be much less demand for US dollars around the globe, so interest rates will skyrocket. Instead of getting a mortgage at today's incredibly low rates of 4.5%, it might cost you 8% or even 10% or 15%. Imagine what that would do to housing prices!

Stock prices will likely plummet by at least 40% in a matter of weeks as a result of this event in the currency markets. It will cost every American business A LOT more money for supplies and materials. No one will be able to get a loan...and no bank will want to make loans. In short, when the US dollar loses its spot as the world's "reserve currency," it will cause a brutal downturn in the economy, which I expect will be about 10-times [sic] worse than the mortgage crisis of 2008.

You see, what will also happen as a result of this currency crisis, and the end of the US dollar as the world's reserve currency, will be massive inflation, the likes of which we have never seen before. When everyone is trying to get rid of their dollars, the government is printing more and more to pay debts, and no one wants to own them, the crisis will reach epic proportions. Just look for example, at what happened to one European country that faced this type of crisis in the 1990s.... This is what happens during a major hyperinflation in the real world. By the early 1990s, the national government of one European nation had spent nearly all its savings. So what did they do next? Simple... they began to steal the savings of private citizens by limiting people's access to their money in government-controlled banks.

And of course, to finance the daily operations of maintaining their basic infrastructure, they started printing money, big time. Even so, the country's basic infrastructure began to fall apart. There were potholes in the street, broken water pipes...elevators that never got repaired...and entire construction projects that simply shut down, before being completed. At this point, the unemployment rate was more than 30%.

Not too bad, right? But it got worse...much worse. You see, once you start down the dangerous road of printing money, things can get extremely bad, very quickly. As San Jose State University Economics Professor Dr. Thayer Watkins, an expert on countries that try to inflate their way out of big debts, wrote on this particular disaster: "The government tried to counter the inflation by imposing price controls. But when inflation continued, the government price controls made the price producers were getting so ridiculously low that they simply stopped producing. Bakers stopped making bread...slaughterhouses refused to sell meat to the stores...other stores closed down" So what did the government do next to try to curb inflation? Well, one bright idea they had was to force stores to fill out government documents every time they increased prices. They thought that this would slow down price increases, because the paperwork would take so much time!

But like many government plans, this one had terrible, unintended consequences. Since stores had to dedicate an employee to do nothing but register this paperwork, and since the process took so long, stores began to raise prices on basic goods at even higher rates, so that they didn't have to come back and file more paperwork! Incredible, isn't it?

Then, of course the government did what all governments do during periods of hyperinflation: They created a new currency...which basically removed six zeroes from the old one. So 100,000,000 old units were soon worth 100 new units. Of course, this didn't work either...it never does. Between October of 1993 and January 1995, prices increase by, get this: 5 quadrillion percent. That's...5,000,000,000,000,000%.

In other words, a loaf of bread that cost $1 in 1993, suddenly cost $50,000,000,000,001..... [*sic*] Yes, that's $50 TRILLION. I know, it's laughable...but I can guarantee that the people of this once proud European country weren't laughing one bit, especially those living on a fixed income. Of course, at this point, the country completely fell apart. As Dr. Thayer Watkins wrote: "The social structure began to collapse. Thieves robbed hospitals and clinics of scarce pharmaceuticals and then sold them in front of the same places they robbed. The railway workers went on strike and closed down the country's rail system."

At this point, businesses and citizens across the country basically refused to take the local currency. Instead, everyone started dealing in German Marks. Keep in mind, the daily rate of inflation was nearly 100%. Can you imagine the panic in a society when the price of just about everything doubles...every single day? It was absolute pandemonium, and the economy basically came to a grinding halt. It was like living in a war zone. Truckers stopped delivering goods. Stores, restaurants, and gas stations all shut down.

In fact, the only way to get gas was to buy it on the side of the road, from someone selling it out of a plastic can. Steve Hanke, an Economics professor at Johns Hopkins, wrote that: "People couldn't afford to buy food in the free market—they kept from starving by either waiting in long lines at state stores for irregularly supplied rations of low-quality staples, or by relying on relatives who lived in the countryside. For long periods, all [the] gas stations were closed, with the exception of one station that catered to foreigners and embassy personnel. People also spent an inordinate amount of time at the foreign-exchange black markets, where they traded huge piles of near-worthless money for a single German mark or US dollar note."

The number of operating busses dropped by 60%...and busses were so crowded that drivers couldn't even collect fares. Government ordered blackouts left people without heat and electricity for long periods of time.

In another ridiculous government move, they actually made it illegal to NOT accept a personal check. Imagine...you could write a check...and in the several days that it typically takes for a check to clear, inflation would wipe out almost all of the cost of covering your check. Of course, as is typical, the government took none of the blame. As Dr. Thayer Watkins reported, the government's official position was that the hyperinflation occurred "because of the unjustly implemented sanctions against the people and state."

Again...I know what you are thinking..."just because it happened in Europe doesn't it mean it can happen here, right"? Well guess what.... The same thing that happened in this European country—Yugoslavia—also just happened in Iceland and Greece, but on a less dramatic scale. Of course, the only reason the situations in Greece and Iceland weren't worse is because of giant foreign bailouts. Yes...that's right...more debt to solve the problem of already existing, insurmountable debts.

It's all going to come to a head soon. Much sooner than most people think.

Remember too that in roughly the past 100 years this type of debt crisis has reared its ugly head in Germany, Russia, Austria, Poland, Argentina, Brazil, Chile, Poland, the Ukraine, Japan, and China. And I believe it will soon happen right here in the United States. Don't believe me? Well, the truth is that it's already happening at the local and state levels. Take a look....

According to the Center on Budget and Policy Priorities, a Washington, D.C.-based think-tank, at least 46 states face huge budget shortfalls for 2011, on top of the deficits they still haven't completely figured out for 2010. The center reports that the total state budget shortfall could reach $160 billion. And although many states got federal help over the past year, that aid is now gone. So what are these desperate governments trying to do?

You probably won't believe their proposals....

* SELL EVERYTHING: The state of Arizona, for example, announced in early 2010 that it is selling $735 million worth of government-owned buildings, but will still occupy them by paying a 20-year lease. The government is selling the legislative buildings, the House and Senate, the State Capitol Executive Tower, the state fairgrounds, even prisons.

* RELEASE PRISONERS: In California, the state has taken the radical step of opening its prison doors and releasing thousands of inmates. About 11% of the state budget ($8 billion) goes to the penal system (more than they spend on higher education). So California is slashing the number of inmates by 6,500 next year. In other words, they are cutting loose about 4% of the prison population. Incredibly, other states, including New York, may soon do the same thing.

* LIFE INSURANCE: In Georgia, the government is proposing taking out "dead peasant" policies on state employees. When these folks die, the money won't go to the dead person's family...but to the state coffers, to help pay for more programs, insurance, and pension liabilities. It's simply incredible, isn't it? State and municipal governments are so broke, and so desperate, that they are taking unprecedented steps to at least temporarily avoid bankruptcy. Nearly every state in the union is talking about legalizing some form of gambling, to boost tax revenue. California still wants to legalize marijuana, even though it was defeated in the recent election.

Of course, none of these ridiculous steps will work on the long run. And the truly amazing thing is that the US Federal government is in even worse shape than the local governments! The only reason we haven't seen the full brunt of this crisis yet on the federal level is because we've just continued to pile on more and more debt. The states can't print money...but the Federal government can (at least for now). And for the moment, this is all that is preventing a currency collapse of unprecedented proportions.

And this is the important point: What most people don't realize is that the US government can only continue printing dollars... as long as the US dollar remains the world's reserve currency.

THE COMING BANKING HOLIDAY

In other words, this is all going to fall apart much sooner than people think. In fact, it's already happening.... The first steps are already well underway. It is happening right now...before our very eyes. *I can't stress this enough:* You need to act now in order to protect your assets, and grow your savings in the next few years. In the next few minutes, I'm going to show you exactly how I'm protecting my own money, and what I recommend doing with your own.

But first, let me show you what exactly is going on right now... "America...must be very worried[.]" Like I said, most Americans don't believe the US dollar could ever lose its spot as the world's reserve currency. But I am here to tell you... this process is already well underway. For example, although it went almost completely unreported in the US press, last fall, a group of the world's most powerful countries, including China, Japan, Russia, and France, got together for a secret meeting—WITHOUT the United States being present or even knowing about the meeting.

Veteran Middle East report Robert Fisk reported on this even in the [*sic*] Britain's Independent newspaper: "In the most profound financial change in recent Middle East history, Gulf Arabs are planning—along with China, Russia, Japan and France—to end dollar dealings for oil, moving instead to a basket of currencies including the Japanese Yen, Chinese yuan, the euro, gold and a new, unified currency planned for nations in the Gulf Cooperation Council, including Saudi Arabia, Abu Dhabi, Kuwait and Qatar."

Fisk also interviewed a Chinese banker who said: "These plans will change the face of international financial transactions. America and Britain must be very worried. You will know how worried by the thunder of denials this news will generate." And sure enough, after Fisk published the details of this secret meet-

11: PORTER STANSBERRY'S STERN MESSAGE

ing, US officials and central bankers from around the globe denied these plans. But as the old central banking adage goes... how do you know exactly when a currency will be devalued? The answer: Right AFTER the head of the central bank goes on television to adamantly deny that any such transaction will occur. (And guess who just went public in recent weeks with a statement about how the US will "not devalue its currency"? Yes, you guessed it...US Treasury Secretary Tim Geithner.)

You see, the last thing a central banker wants to do in the midst of devaluation is to give people a warning BEFORE he can devalue. So they have to deny, deny, deny. After the announcement is made, it's too late for citizens and investors to get out. Like I said, what's incredible is that this story of a secret meeting among most of the major powers besides the US was greatly under reported in the American press. But you know what...the way I see it, it's much more telling to look at actions rather than government press releases.

For example, here is what is happening, right now in the real world. When you read these facts, I think you'll agree with me that the US dollar's days are numbered, as far as remaining the world's reserve currency.

China is getting out. Cheng Siwei, a former vice-chairman of the Standing Committee, said that China is going to stop putting so much money into US dollars, and will instead look to the Japanese Yen and the Euro. China holds more US dollars than anyone else on the planet. But China is getting out of the US dollar as fast as they can without crashing their own economy.

Look at this chart....

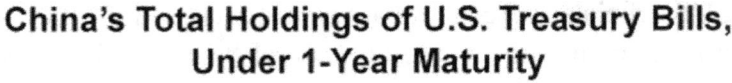

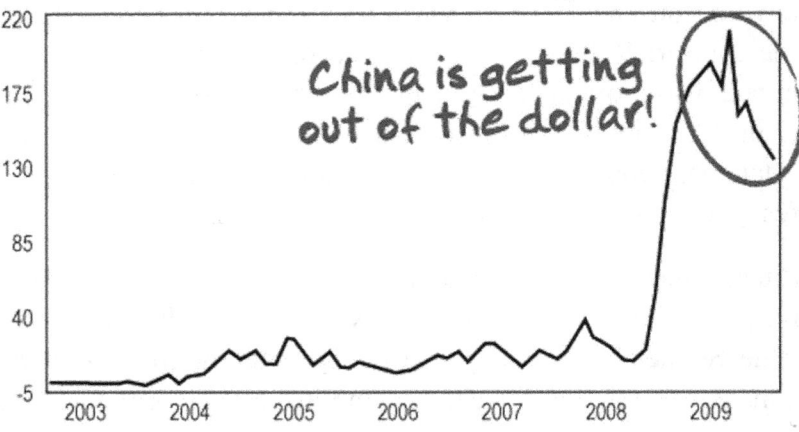

It shows that China's holdings of US dollars peaked in 2009, but China is unloading as many dollars as they can, as quickly as possible. And this is just one sign of the end of the US dollar standard. There are many more.... The dollar is no longer good here. As I am sure you are aware, for years the US dollar has been accepted almost universally around the globe. Heck, many times when I've traveled, I never even bothered to convert to the local currency, because I knew everyone would take my dollars. Well, that's simply not the case anymore.... HSBC, one of the largest banks in Mexico, no longer allows you to deposit US dollars into their banks. They've done this on the heels of money-laundering allegations, but we suspect they also simply don't want to be stuck with tons of US dollars, as the currency continues to decline. This move would have been unfathomable 10 years ago...that a big bank in Mexico would no longer accept US dollars for deposit. But today it is the harsh reality.

And Mexico is not the only place this is occurring.... Reuters reports that the same thing has happened in 2008 in one of

Europe's most popular tourist spots.... Currency exchange outlets in Amsterdam have been reportedly turning away customers who want to exchange their US dollars for Euros. As one traveling American told the Reuters news agency: "Our dollar is worth maybe zero over here," said Mary Kelly, an American tourist from Indianapolis, Indiana, in front of the Anne Frank house. "It's hard to find a place to exchange. We have to go downtown, to the central station or post office."

In India, the country's tourism minister said in 2008 that US dollars will no longer be accepted at the country's heritage tourist sites, like the Taj Mahal. And the US dollar is no longer good anywhere in Cuba. The *New York Times* reports that: "now, many shops in China no longer accept dollar-based credit cards issued by foreign banks...and foreigners cannot convert American dollars into renminbi beyond a given quota."

Iran, of course, has already moved all of its reserves out of US dollars, and Kuwait de-pegged it's currency from the dollar a few years ago: Bloomberg News recently reported that China and Russia plan to start trading in each other's currencies to diminish the dollar's role in global trade. "Given the risk to the dollar and US assets from their fiscal position, they want to reduce their dependence on the dollar as an invoicing currency," said Bhanu Baweja, of UBS bank. It's even happening here in the USA. Most Americans don't know that some states in the Mid-West are already using "alternative currencies"....

An NBC News affiliate in Michigan reports that "new types of money are popping up across Mid-Michigan and supporters say, it's not counterfeit, but rather a competing currency. Right now, for example, you can buy a meal or visit a chiropractor without using actual US legal tender." What most Americans don't realize is that this is all totally legal. The US Treasury Dept web site says that, according to Coinage Act of 1965: "There is... no Federal statute mandating that a private business, a person or an organization must accept currency or coins as for payment for goods and/or services." I saw one report that says there are now 150 of these alternative local US currencies being accepted around the country!

USA Today reports that the largest of these local currencies is a currency called "Berkshares," which are being used in the Berkshires region of western Massachusetts. According to the paper:

"Since its start in 2006, the system, the largest of its kind in the country, has circulated $2.3 million worth of BerkShares. And even in places that do not yet have local currencies, store owners may now actually prefer foreign currencies rather than US dollars.... In Washington, DC, just 25 miles from my office, some stores have begun accepting euros. Of course, the euro isn't much more stable than the dollar right now. But my point is that most people don't understand there is NO FEDERAL REQUIREMENT in the United States for a private store to accept dollars for non-debt transactions."

You see, no matter what the government decides, stores and businesses will accept whatever they believe is a strong currency. As Texas Representative Ron Paul wrote recently: "If you walk into a 7-11 to buy a soda, the clerk doesn't have to accept your dollars, he could demand euros, silver, or copper. But because legal tender laws backing the dollar have caused the dollar to drive other currencies out of circulation, [right now] it is easier for stores to accept dollars." Well, all that is quickly changing....

Many places in Texas now accept Mexican pesos for payment. "Euros Accepted" signs are popping up in of all places: Manhattan. And not only Manhattan, but in New York's favorite summer playground...the Hamptons. There, an art gallery assistant was

11: PORTER STANSBERRY'S STERN MESSAGE

quoted by *The Real Deal:* "I wouldn't want to discourage a sale in any way because of a currency issue." And it's not just small stores that are accepting other methods of payment besides US dollars. The Chicago mercantile exchange the world's largest futures and commodities exchange board), now accepts gold to settle futures contracts. Until recently, the exchange typically accepted only US treasuries and bonds as payment.

These guys obviously see the writing on the wall. This would have all been completely unthinkable 10 years ago, but today it's a reality. And this trend is going to keep moving incredibly fast. That is why.... The smartest investors are taking action... Bill Gross, who probably knows as much about currencies and debt as anyone in the world, runs the world's biggest bond fund. He was quoted by Bloomberg:

"We've told all of our clients that if you only had one idea, one investment, it would be to buy an investment in a non-dollar currency. That should be on top of the list." Jim Rogers, one of the world's most successful multi-millionaire investors[,] writes: "The dollar is not just in decline; it's a mess. If something isn't done soon, I believe the dollar could lose its status as the world's reserve currency and medium of exchange, something that would lead to a huge decline in the standard of living for US citizens like nothing we've seen in nearly a century."

I know... you probably still don't believe it can happen here in the United States. But think about it.... Are we as Americans really immune to the laws of economics and finance? I don't think so. And every circumstance I know of, in which a government has tried to inflate its debts away, has ended in disaster. It will happen here too. As Jim Rogers says:

"History teaches us that such imprudent monetary and fiscal behavior has always led to economic disaster." This is why World

Bank president, Robert B. Zoellick, in a speech at the School for Advanced International Studies at Johns Hopkins University, recently said: "The United States would be mistaken to take for granted the dollar's place as the world's predominant reserve currency. Looking forward, there will increasingly be other options to the dollar."

And this is why the International Monetary Fund (IMF) recently published a paper calling for a new global world currency. A paper entitled "Reserve Accumulation and International Monetary Stability," written by the Strategy, Policy and Review Department of the IMF, recommends that the world adopt a global currency called the "Bancor" with a global central bank to administer the currency. The report is dated April 13, 2010...and no, unfortunately this is not just a bad rumor. This is a deadly serious proposal in an official document from one of most powerful institutions in the world.

Do you see where this is all heading? As Brazilian economist and strategist Ricardo C. Amaral wrote: "The US dollar served its purpose since the end of WW II and became the major foreign exchange reserve currency... [but] the days of the US dollar playing that special role... has reached the end of the line, since today that system is very sick and it is dying a slow death.... Mr. Amaral added that we will soon see: "the major collapse of the US dollar creating the biggest international monetary crisis the world has ever seen...."

This is why gold and silver prices are soaring:

11: PORTER STANSBERRY'S STERN MESSAGE

It's not a matter of "if" the US dollar will lose its status as the world's reserve currency...it's simply a matter of "when." Investors know there are serious, serious problems with the US dollar, so they are fleeing to precious metals, which have historically been very reliable when a country has major currency problems. In short: It's not hard to see why people are no longer accepting US dollars... and why many foreign countries are pushing for a new world reserve currency.

The good news is, no matter what happens, I've found several ways for you to protect your savings—and you could even make 3- to 5-times your money over the next few years. I'll show you exactly what to do in a moment. But first let me explain why the collapse of the dollar as the world's reserve currency could happen much sooner than most people expect....

The REAL State of the US Economy

I know many of my friends, colleagues, and family members are still in serious denial. In the world of psychology, they call this the "normalcy bias."

You see, the normalcy bias actually refers to our natural reactions when facing a crisis. The normalcy bias causes smart people to underestimate the possibility of a disaster and its effects. In short: People believe that since something has *never* happened before... it *never will*. We are all guilty of it...it's just human nature. The normalcy bias also makes people unable to deal with a disaster, once it has occurred. Basically...people have a really hard time preparing for and dealing with something they have never experienced. The normalcy bias often results in unnecessary deaths in disaster situations. For example, think about the Jewish populations of World War II....

As Barton Biggs reports in his book, *Wealth, War, and Wisdom:* "By the end of 1935, 100,000 Jews had left Germany, but 450,000 still [remained]. Wealthy Jewish families...kept thinking and hoping that the worst was over....

Many of the German Jews, brilliant, cultured, and cosmopolitan as they were, were too complacent. They had been in Germany so long and were so well established, they simply couldn't believe there was going to be a crisis that would endanger them. They were too comfortable. They believed the Nazi's anti-Semitism was an episodic event and that Hitler's bark was worse than his bite. [They] reacted sluggishly to the rise of Hitler for completely understandable but tragically erroneous reasons. Events moved much faster than they could imagine."

This is one of the most tragic examples of the devastating effects of the "normalcy bias" the world has ever seen. Just think about

11: PORTER STANSBERRY'S STERN MESSAGE

what was going on at the time. Jews were arrested, beaten, taxed, robbed, and jailed for no reason other than the fact that they practiced a particular religion. As a result, they were shipped off to concentration camps. Their houses and businesses were seized. Yet most Jews STILL didn't leave Nazi Germany, because they simply couldn't believe that things would get as bad as they did. That's the normalcy bias...with devastating results. We saw the same thing happen during Hurricane Katrina.... Even as it became clear that the levee system was not going to work, tens of thousands of people stayed in their homes, directly in the line of the oncoming waves of water.

People had never seen things get this bad before...so they simply didn't believe it could happen. As a result, nearly 2,000 residents died. Again...it's the "normalcy bias." We simply refuse to see the evidence that's right in front of our face, because it is unlike anything we have experienced before.

The normalcy bias kicks in...and we continue to go about our lives as if nothing is unusual or out of the ordinary. Well, we're seeing the same thing happen in the United States right now. We have been the world's most powerful country for nearly 100 years. The US dollar has reigned supreme as the world's reserve currency for more than 50 years. Most of us in America simply cannot fathom these things changing. But I promise you this: Things are changing...and faster than most people realize.

For a moment, just look at a tiny fraction of the evidence around us....

*** 13% OF POPULATION ON FOODSTAMPS*

And get this: The number of Americans on food stamps has now gone up every month for 37 months. That's over three years! Can a country really be in good shape when 14% of the population can't even afford to buy food?

THE COMING BANKING HOLIDAY

Or how about this...

**SHANTY TOWNS COMING TO YOUR NEIGHBORHOOD

Although it's gone almost completely unreported in the mainstream press, in a dozen or so cities across the nation (like Fresno, Sacramento, and Nashville), there are hundreds of people living in modern-day, Depression-era shanty towns. The Fresno shanty town has received the most publicity, after a visit by Oprah Winfrey. There, about 2,000 residents are homeless. They even have a security desk at the shelter, because the encampment has gotten so large. City officials say they have three major encampments near downtown, and smaller settlements along two local highways.

Also...

**43% OF AMERICAN FAMILIES ARE ESSENTIALLY BROKE

According to a recent article on MSN Money, about 43% of the American families spend more than they earn each year. Look at this chart...it's unbelievable.

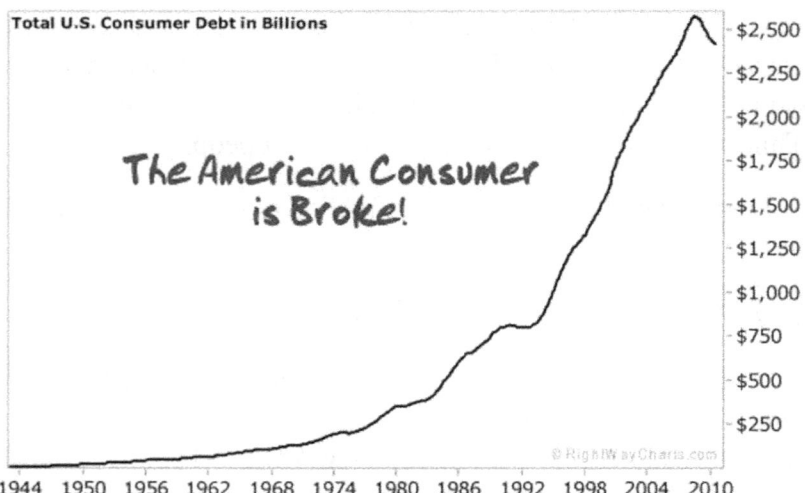

11: PORTER STANSBERRY'S STERN MESSAGE

The average household carries $8,000 in credit card debt...and personal bankruptcies have doubled in the past decade. How in the world can we possibly spend our way out of the current crisis? We certainly can't do it with savings...the only answer is to print more money, which will hasten the fall of the US dollar as the world's reserve currency.

** *THE MYSTERY OF DISAPPEARING JOBS*

There's simply no one better at bending statistics than the US government. Take the unemployment rate, for example. Back in the 1930s, anyone without a job but not retired was considered "unemployed." Today, however, the government calculates unemployment mainly by counting the number of people receiving unemployment benefits. So when people's benefits expire, they are no longer counted...and the unemployment rate actually falls! Ridiculous...I know.

But the reality is, the true unemployment rate is much, much higher than what the government is reporting.

If you don't believe me, look at two job postings I read about recently....

In Long Island City, an estimated 2,000 people waited in line at the local employment office—some for as long as four days!—to apply for 100 elevator mechanic apprenticeship positions. And in Massillon, Ohio, 700 people applied for a single janitorial job...paying $16 an hour, plus benefits! The point is, our country is not growing jobs, because the government makes it harder and harder for businesses. With current regulations in place, our country will never experience the type of growth necessary to dig our government out of the hole they've put themselves in.

I'm sure you think I'm exaggerating, but just look at what the CEO of one of America's most important companies said.. [*sic*] Intel CEO Paul Otellini said in a recent speech: "I can tell you definitively that it costs $1 billion more per factory for me to build, equip, and operate a semiconductor manufacturing facility in the United States" He said that 90% of the additional costs are not from higher labor rates...but from higher taxes and regulatory charges, which other nations simply don't impose.

Cypress Semiconductor CEO T.J. Rodgers agreed that the problem is not higher US wages, but anti-business laws. He was quoted in an interview with CNET News: "The killer factor in California for a manufacturer to create, say, a thousand blue-collar jobs is a hostile government that doesn't want you there and demonstrates it in thousands of ways."

Few Americans today realize that we have *the second highest corporate tax rate in the world.* And since Japan's new prime minister just announced that he plans to reduce the country's corporate tax rate by 15%...the US could soon have THE highest corporate tax rate in the world. Why would anyone want to start a business here, when they can do it for less money...and keep more of the money they make...by locating elsewhere? It's just another good reason to avoid the US dollar.... So is this:

** DEBT-RIDDEN US COMPANIES

Did you know that in 1979, there were 61 American companies that earned a top-level AAA credit rating from Moody's? Today, there are only four: Automatic Data Processing, Exxon, Johnson & Johnson, and Microsoft. Does this sound like an economic recovery to you...when only four companies in the entire country are stable enough to earn a triple-A credit rating? Me neither. But it's nothing compared to what's going on in the housing sector....

** A CRAZY LAS VEGAS ECONOMICS STORY

You want to know how crazy things are in the US right now... Consider the bizarre state of the Las Vegas housing market, where The *New York Times* reports that building is booming again in a city where nearly 10,000 new houses are empty, thousands are in foreclosure, thousands of regular people have simply stopped paying their mortgages and average prices are down more than 60% since 2006.

What could possibly be driving this building mania? Well, it turns out that buyers don't want homes that were built during the boom, because they sit in neighborhoods that look like ghost towns, and because many of these never-occupied houses are filled with cockroaches and other critters. So local builders are doing the worst possible thing they could be doing in Las Vegas right now...building more homes! Similar scenarios are taking shape in Phoenix and other US cities. Of course, this might look good for economic numbers, but all it does is make the situation much, much worse in the long run.

Want to see another crazy trick some businesses are using to artificially boost their earnings numbers? This is just incredible to me....

** OUR HOPE FOR THE FUTURE: NEW JERSEY'S HOMELESS

If you've been reading my work at all over the past few years, you know that I am extremely bearish on the "for profit" education sector, such as University of Phoenix. What could possibly be wrong with these institutions that offer inexpensive education to tens of thousands of students across the country? Well, to me it's just another symptom of how distorted and crazy our economy and country has become. Here's what I mean.... One of the crazy practices institutions employ is to actually enroll homeless people into their programs.

You probably think I'm making this up...but even *Business Week* recently ran a report on this practice. Why would they do this? Well, because these folks qualify for federal grants and loans used to pay for college tuition fees. According to reports I read, the University of Phoenix, for instance, relies on federal funds for more than 85% of its revenues. At another for-profit school, Drake College of Business, almost 5% of the student body at its Newark, N.J., campus is homeless, *Business Week* recently reported. Of course, the majority of these students will never be able to repay their loans. But the colleges certainly don't care...that's the government's problem...not theirs. Once again, it's the taxpayers like you and me who will be left holding the bag. And here's another good reason why investors are afraid of holding dollars right now....

11: PORTER STANSBERRY'S STERN MESSAGE

** IN THE STOCK MARKET, IT'S 1937 ALL OVER AGAIN

One of the most worrisome problems in the stock market right now is that we could basically be repeating the exact same situation that occurred from 1937 to 1942. Most Americans think we've had this amazing stock market recovery since the financial crisis of 2008...and we have to a certain extent. But we are by no means out of the woods. In fact, during America's last real economic collapse, in the 1930s and 1940s, we saw a similar drop and recovery...before the markets crashed all over again.

In fact, the situation is eerily similar. Look at this chart...it's one of the scariest I've seen in a long time. It shows an overlay of what happened in the stock market in 1937 compared to 2008.

In both situations, we saw big crashes, of about the exact same magnitude...then a big recovery, again of about the same size. But what will happen next?

165

THE COMING BANKING HOLIDAY

Well, if history is any guide, we could well have another big leg down in the stock market. That's exactly what happened 70 years ago. And with all of the problems left unresolved in our economy today, it could certainly happen again, especially if the US dollar loses its reserve status.

As *The Wall Street Journal* reported: "Over the last year the stock market has followed a path eerily similar to 1937. First, a strong, rapid run to a recovery high—same pace, same magnitude. Then a correction—again, the same. Will we continue on the path that led the correction of 1937 into a collapse in 1938? The point is, the cards are seriously stacked against us. This looming currency crisis is inevitable. Almost every state in the country is on the verge of bankruptcy. We have borrowed an impossible amount of money, which we'll never be able to pay back.["]

Our economy is an absolute mess. Taxes are sky high already... and will certainly go much higher over the next few years. And nearly all of the world's major financial players are preparing for an alternative to the US dollar as the world's reserve currency. To me, it is so obvious that we are about to experience a serious currency crisis, that I can't believe people can deny this reality with a straight face. Again, if you don't believe a currency crisis is coming, just glance back at the previous gold and silver chart, showing it's comparison to the US dollar over the past decade.

It's obvious that smart investors want to hold gold and silver, not US dollars. Anyone with any sense or basic understanding of economics can tell that the US dollar is doomed. And it's going to have major repercussions, which the average American has not yet even considered. So, what can you do? Well, I've done a lot of research on this, and have found that there are a surprising number of simple things you can do to not only protect what you've currently got, but to also potentially make quite a bit of money as this currency crisis unfolds.

11: PORTER STANSBERRY'S STERN MESSAGE

Here's what I recommend....

What You Can Do to Protect Yourself and Actually Make Money

So what should you do... to protect and possibly even grow your wealth in the next few years? Well, there's a series of pretty simple financial moves I believe you should begin making, immediately. And here's something I want you to keep in mind: I'm really only going to talk about your finances here.

As far as protecting your family...well...it depends on your circumstances. If you live in an urban area, I recommend making sure you've got somewhere you can go in case there are riots or food and water shortages. I think there's a very good chance we'll see that in the next two years. Wherever you're going to wait out the chaos, I recommend you have basic food, water, and medical supplies to last you for at least six months. Remember, you won't be able to count on the government during this crisis. Think about it...if the government couldn't even save the city of New Orleans during hurricane Katrina, how in the world will it save an entire country when all hell breaks lose?

And as I said earlier, the truth is, the government won't even try to save individual American citizens...the government will be much more concerned with saving itself. As far as taking care of your money—to make sure you don't lose money and even use this situation to come out quite a bit ahead—well, that's where I can help you. All of the moves I recommend are simple and fairly straightforward to implement—at least right now. If you wait to do these things, however, they will almost certainly get very expensive, difficult, and even impossible to do.

If you do these things now, not only will you be better prepared to weather the coming storm, I believe you could also make quite a bit of money over the next few years. And if I'm wrong... well...that's the best part...I think you'll still make very good

THE COMING BANKING HOLIDAY

gains. Even if all we get out of this crisis is a mild inflation, you will still be set up to do very, very well.

So here are the specific steps you should take....

STEP #1. GET SOME OF YOUR MONEY BEYOND THE REACH OF THE US GOVERNMENT (it's perfectly legal, and a lot easier than you think)

I know you probably don't believe me when I tell you that the US government is going to implement policies to save itself, which are unimaginable right now. But remember, desperate governments will do very desperate things. That's why they outlawed the ownership of gold 80 years ago. That's why they are already talking about "nationalizing" automatic 401(k) and retirement plans...and it's why it might soon be against the law to open a foreign bank account, or to move your money overseas without paying outrageous taxes. The good news is, I met recently with a man who is considered one of the top "asset protection" attorneys in America.

In short, I learned that there are four simple investments you can make right now, which you DO NOT have to report to the US government. Don't get me wrong.... When and if you ever sell these things, years down the road, you are still required to pay taxes on your gains. But the great thing is, while you are holding these investments, so long as you play by the rules, neither you nor anyone else is required to report them to the government.

And this benefit should be obvious.... The less the government knows about where you have your money, the better. They simply will have a very hard time taking what they don't know you have. I am personally putting a fairly significant portion of my portfolio into one of these assets. And I plan to hold it for a long time. No matter what happens, I know I'll have a significant amount of money that is beyond the government's grasp..

11: PORTER STANSBERRY'S STERN MESSAGE

STEP #2: ACQUIRE THE WORLD'S SAFEST ASSETS, WHICH ARE LIKELY TO PERFORM BEST DURING THIS PERIOD.

What I'm talking about here is buying as much gold and silver as you can reasonably afford. I know...gold has had a huge run, jumping more than 400% in the past decade. But believe me, when the US dollar loses its status as the world's reserve currency, this early run is going to be a mere afterthought. I will be surprised if gold does not reach $5,000 or $6,000 an ounce in the next few years.

The smartest money managers in the world, people like George Soros, David Einhorn, and John Paulson, have all recently taken huge positions in gold. And I think you are crazy to not do the same. And what about silver? Well, I believe silver will serve a unique role during this currency crisis. Let me explain....

For most of recorded history, the price of gold has been around 16 times the price of silver. This ratio—the so-called "silver ratio"—has fluctuated from time to time based on silver discoveries and attempts by governments to regulate the silver-to-gold ratio. But... in a free market, where demand for silver as money exists, I'd expect the natural supply and demand balance to lead to a silver price around 1/16 times the price of gold.

If gold = $1,400..... [sic] Silver should = $87, but today it's around $34.

Based on the historical ratio, with the price of gold around $1,500, the price of silver should be around $90. It's not, of course. Today, silver is trading around $34. Today then, gold is selling for more than 44-times the price of silver. What explains the difference between hundreds of years of history and today? Why is silver still so cheap relative to gold? When silver is "de-monetized," as it is now (meaning it's not being used for money, but just for industrial purposes), supplies soar as people sell silver for gold and other currencies.

On the other hand, during periods of monetary crisis, demand for silver as money pushes the silver ratio heavily in silver's favor. For example, the ratio returned to its historic range (16) during World War I. It happened again in the early 1970s, when Nixon abandoned the gold standard. It also happened most famously in 1979-1980, when it seemed as if America was really entering a serious money crisis. Most people don't know this, but silver is actually the best-performing asset of this century...not gold.

As my multimillionaire friend and currency expert Chris Weber pointed out, Gold has risen from $256 to $1,500 since 2001. That is a rise of over 500%. Silver has risen from $4.02 to $34. That is a rise of 845%. In short, silver is the best hedge against a money crisis. As the dollar fails, silver will once again be in demand as money. And my friend Chris Weber believes silver will likely hit $187 an ounce. If that happens, you could make gains of around 450% if you invest at today's prices. But I have to tell you, right now, I am really worried that a lot of our subscribers and many, many hard-working Americans are going to get caught totally by surprise when this inevitable crisis hits.

Remember: The government is not going to save you. If the government couldn't save one small city from the disastrous news coming, then how is it going to save all of us when the [beep] really hits the fan? You can either let things happen to you...or you can take a few simple steps and take charge of your family's fate. For additional information, go to www.StansberryResearch.com.

Please, just give the work I've done a look...and I believe you will have all the information you need at your disposal.

Courtesy of Porter Stansberry, Stansberry & Associates Investment Research.

11: PORTER STANSBERRY'S STERN MESSAGE

Our comment: Porter does not pull any punches here; he tells it as he sees it. I agree with him that America is in bad shape financially and politically. He raises public concern like no one else can and, because of this, his essay fits the book nicely. I like the part about silver being the best investment when "it" hits, and I also like the part about keeping a low profile from the government. He writes an informative and futuristic newsletter, which I subscribe to.

Our action: We are deeply concerned about the financial situation in America, as are most of our friends and clients. We do believe in keeping a low profile and storing precious metals, especially silver.

CHAPTER TWELVE

John Williams: The Coming Hyper-Inflation

"The government is good at one thing. It knows how to break your legs, and then hand you a crutch and say, 'See if it weren't for the government, you wouldn't be able to walk.'"

—Harry Browne

THE COMING BANKING HOLIDAY

The official inflation rate, as of January 2012, was 2.93% (according to InflationData.com). However, every person who drives and eats knows that it is much higher. While Californians are up in arms at their gasoline prices almost hitting $5 a gallon, we here in NZ pay $9.44. It costs us $5 in gas here on Waiheke Island to buy a $4.50 cup of coffee at the beach each morning.

Retirees not only see their savings accounts paying virtually zero, but they now face serious inflation. I was listening to the weekly "McAlvany Commentary" recently (don't miss it, by the way), and John Williams was guesting. He's our favorite statistician, and he sure didn't disappoint. Not only did he do one interview, but two.

However, before the interview, he appeared on King World News, and issued the following warning:

"The US economic and systemic-solvency crises of the last five years continue to deteriorate. Yet they remain just the precursors to the coming Great Collapse: a hyperinflationary great depression. The unfolding circumstance will encompass a complete loss in the purchasing power of the US dollar; a collapse in the normal stream of US commercial and economic activity; a collapse in the US financial system, as we know it; and a likely realignment of the US political environment."

John Williams continues: "Outside timing on the hyperinflation remains 2014, but events of the last year have accelerated the movement towards this ultimate dollar catastrophe. Following Mr. Bernanke's extraordinary efforts to debase the US currency in late 2010, the dollar had lost its traditional safe-haven status by early 2011. Whatever global confidence had remained behind the U.S dollar was lost in July and August (2011)."

That was in response to the lack of political will—shown by those who control the White House and Congress—to address the long-range insolvency of the US government, and as a result of the later credit-rating downgrade to US Treasury debt.

Those latter circumstances triggered something of dollar selling panic, particularly as reflected in the corresponding buying of gold and Swiss francs, but various interventions, misdirection and manipulations helped to quell the currency disorders. Still, many financial markets were left rocking with the aftershocks of a major shift in the global view of the US dollar.

The economy has underperformed and likely will continue to underperform consensus forecasts by a significant margin. In turn, weaker-than-expected economic growth will mean significantly worse-than-expected federal budget deficits, Treasury funding needs and banking-system solvency conditions.

With the US election just seven months off, political pressures will mount to favor fiscal stimulus measures instead of restraint. The Fed should be forced to provide new "easing" in an effort to continue propping the banking system (the explanation will be an effort to boost the economy). Given the Treasury's funding needs, the easing likely will in the form of renewed buying of US Treasuries, with the Fed remaining lender of last resort there.

Consistent with the precedent set in 2008, the Fed, and likely the Treasury, also will remain in place to do whatever is needed, at whatever cost, to prevent systemic collapse in the United States. All of these actions, though, have costs in terms of higher domestic inflation and intensified dollar debasement.

The US dollar remains highly vulnerable to massive, panicked selling, at any time, with little or no warning. The next round of Federal Reserve or US government easing or stimulus could be the proximal trigger for such a currency panic and/or for strong efforts to strip the US currency of its global reserve currency status.

As the advance squalls from this great financial tempest come ashore, the government could be expected to launch a variety of efforts at forestalling the hyperinflation's landfall, but such efforts will buy little time and ultimately will fail in preventing the dollar's collapse. The timing of the early days—the onset—of full-blown hyperinflation likely will be coincident with a broad global rejection of the US dollar, which, again, could happen at any time.

With no viable or politically-practical way of balancing US fiscal conditions and avoiding this financial economic Armageddon, the best action that individuals can take at this point remains to protect themselves, both as to meeting short-range survival needs as well as to preserving current wealth and assets over the longer term. Efforts there, respectively, would encompass building a store of key consumables, such as food and water, and moving assets into physical precious metals and outside of the US dollar.

Courtesy of Eric King, King World News

Here are John's two interviews with David McAlvany and Keven Orrick. This first "Hyper-inflation" interview took place on January 18, 2012.

MP3 Hyperlink: www.McalvanyWeeklyCommentary.com/wp-content/uploads//ica2012-0118.mp3

12: JOHN WILLIAMS: THE COMING HYPER-INFLATION

David: John, it's great to have you with us. As we begin 2012 we look at a number of factors which are fairly critical. When we look at economic reporting, and the data that is coming out of our different government agencies, there are a few things that stand out here at the beginning of the year. 15.3 trillion is, roughly, our gross domestic product. It is also our national debt, but that is not the sum total of our liabilities. We are now at 100% of GDP, and that is one thing that we want to look at today, some of the big picture issues in terms of our economy, and what some of these economic statistic imply as we look at 2012, 2013, 2014. We are above 90% on the debt-to-GDP level. That has always implied a lower growth environment moving forward, carrying that much debt.

That's not the only issue. We have a lot of things to cover with you today. We want to talk about the deficit, of course. We want to talk about the real deficit, the gap-based federal deficit. We want to talk about employment statistics, where we are, and where you see us going. Some comments on bank lending, and whether or not that will improve, or if we are just going to be stuck in the mud, in terms of velocity. And then maybe just a little bit on the depth and duration of the contraction we have been in, contrary to some perhaps at the NBER who would say we are clearly out of the recession.

We want to cover some of these big-picture points, and have you shed some light for us on the importance of statistics and what they tell us today, as signs and signals of what lies ahead.

John Williams: Well, that's quite a bit, and I am happy to help wherever I can. Where do you want to start?

David: Let's start in with the federal deficit. In 2010 it was 1.299 trillion, and then in 2011 it was virtually the same, 1.294 trillion, and you have pointed out that the gap-based federal deficit is quite a bit higher than that. What is the difference between the headline number that we see advertised, the 1.2, 1.3 trillion number, and the gap-based deficit?

John: The gap-based deficit is based on generally accepted accounting principles, where the government's operations are reported as a large corporation might report its operations. This has been in place now for pretty much well beyond a decade now, in which the Treasury has been publishing these reports. It came out of the efforts back in the 1970s, what were then the big ten accounting firms and Congress, to bring the federal government's operations under better control so people could understand what was happening. Despite all the efforts, the government accountability office, still called the GAO, which does the auditing, won't sign off on the statements because of problems with auditing of the defense department and Homeland Security.

But as it puts all the numbers together, there is an area, which is not widely followed, but it is extremely important in terms of whether or not the nation is solvent, and unfortunately, the nation is not, at least not on a long-term basis. The issue is in terms of the unfunded liabilities for Social Security, Medicare, and such. The way they handle it in the financial statements is that they show the numbers as estimated by the various trust funds, but they reflect it in terms of net present value. Where you have a shortfall of, for example, 20 trillion dollars net present value, that is how much cash you would have to have in hand today, earning money on that going forward to cover that liability.

In terms of the year-to-year change, which would effectively go to the income statement, or would be the net deficit or surplus, depending upon which way it went, instead of being in the area that the government reports for the cash deficit, I think it is in around the 1.3 trillion range, which is extraordinary, in and of itself. We are seeing annual deficits right now of 5 trillion dollars. That is with all the annual change reflected there on an accounting basis for the deterioration in Social Security and Medicare.

David: If it was 1.3, you would say that is really not a sustainable trajectory.

John: 1.3 certainly is not. 5 trillion is beyond any hope. To put that into perspective, if you wanted to, for example, bring the system into balance for one year, let alone make it solvent going forward, you could not raise taxes enough to eliminate the deficit. You could take 100% of everyone's salary and wages and you would still be in deficit. On the spending side, you could cut every penny of government spending except for Social Security and Medicare, and you would still be in deficit.

I get a lot of comments like, "Why are you targeting Social Security? I paid into it." I fully appreciate the feelings. I paid into Social Security, too. The problem is, the system has been expanded by the politicians beyond anything that is sustainable. They cannot conceivably raise enough taxes, or balance the deficit, with the existing political limits on spending, going forward. We are insolvent. We've gotten to a point that the government cannot fund its operations, or borrow enough to fund its operations.

We actually saw that in this last year, a very unusual time where the Federal Reserve, with its Quantitative Easing II package, actually bought, in net Treasury securities, more than the Treasury issued for public consumption, so that the Fed, effectively, in that period of time, fully monetized the federal debt. That is working through the system—very, very inflationary, and we have, unfortunately, a lot more of that ahead.

But if the government can't have normal auctions, if it cannot raise the funds from people who want to lend the money to the government, domestic or foreign, it will most likely do what almost every other country in that type of circumstance has done, and that is, to print the money they need to meet their obligations. That becomes very inflationary—hyperinflationary.

David: That brings us to the point of a report that you put together about a year ago, a hyperinflation Special Report, in 2011. You have updated that with a few data points, and are doing a new release here in the next few days. I will be quite frank. If anyone who listens to our weekly commentary has not read The Special Report because you don't subscribe to Shadow Government Statistics, you are a little out in the cold without a jacket. This is called necessary reading.

The idea, within the 66-page report, which is about to be re-released with all the updates, is essentially, that we are moving toward hyperinflation, and I think, argues, very effectively, that this process which has begun over the last ten years, and became a virtual certainty by 2004, has been accelerated as a result of the financial crisis, and Washington, D.C.'s tinkering with the system, unfortunately, not very effectively.

Maybe you can speak to the acceleration of the process, and some of the dots you are connecting that would imply the inevitable circumstance of hyperinflation here in the US

John: Sure. Before we had the financial crisis that broke in 2007 and 2008, the system was headed for hyperinflation by the end of the current decade, perhaps by 2020. That was just the way the government's obligations were lined up. We were seeing deficits still averaging 5 trillion dollars a year on a gap accounting basis, completely unsustainable. By 2020 we would have been at a point where the government would have had to print the money to meet its obligations. There is no way it could sustain that with borrowing.

12: JOHN WILLIAMS: THE COMING HYPER-INFLATION

We had a circumstance develop in 2006–2007 where the economy started to turn down sharply, particularly in the housing area, which helped to trigger a financial crisis. The economy helped to trigger the financial crisis, the financial crisis exacerbated the downturn in the economy, and we saw almost a collapse in economic activity going through the year 2007, into 2008, even to 2009, and it has been pretty much bottom-bouncing since, irrespective of the official pronouncements out of Washington.

But in August/September of 2008, the people in Washington realized that they had so loused up the system that they were on the brink of a systemic failure, that the banking system was going to collapse if they didn't do something. They weren't kidding about that. We shouldn't have gotten to that point, but having gotten to that point, they had to do what they had to do and put forth all sorts of emergency spending, lending, guarantees—they created whatever money they had to in order to keep the system from failing.

I will contend that they will continue to do that so long as the markets will let them get away with it. The problem is that the cures that they put forth did nothing to resolve the problem. It bought them a little time in terms of systemic stability, but the systemic solvency crisis continues. The banks are not healthy. The big banks are still in trouble.

We have another crisis that is brewing here. The US economy did not recover. It, in fact, is still bottom-bouncing, and it is about to turn down again. All these factors will keep the Fed and the Treasury, the federal government, trying to pump money into the economy, doing some form of stimulus, providing liquidity to the banking system. The costs of all that are very inflationary, and that has accelerated the process whereby, if you look over the last year, the actions taken by the Fed, by the federal government, did a lot to kill global confidence in the US dollar.

Looking back to the events in July/August of last year, they had the negotiation over the debt ceiling, and the inability to come up with a deficit reduction package or the willingness to actually take the political steps necessary to slash the social spending, which is effecting a looming national bankruptcy. As that fell apart, the rest of the world was watching the United States, and if you look at the market reaction, this was even before the downgrade of the US Treasuries, there was panic selling of the dollar. The Swiss franc was soaring, gold was soaring, and that is one of the prerequisites to having hyperinflation—a loss of confidence—a loss of confidence in the dollar.

Then there were all sorts of market interventions. I would contend that the crisis in Europe was a real problem, but there was a lot of effort made to focus market attention on the crisis in Europe as a foil—efforts were made to curtail the rise in gold prices. The Swiss National Bank moved, at least for a short period of time, to tie the Swiss franc to the euro to effectively prop the euro, and to effectively prop the dollar.

It is an unstable, very volatile situation, that could break apart at any time, and as it does, there are a number of things that could push it over the edge, such as renewed Fed action, which is a virtual certainty, just a matter of when it hits. But you will start to see this circumstance move very rapidly to a higher inflation, and then as the confidence in the dollar continues to shrink, into a hyperinflation.

A lot of people say, "Oh, my goodness, how can you have inflation with a weak economy?" Indeed, we have a weak economy, and there are a lot of problems with what is being reported, but if you look at something as simple as payroll employment, despite all the problems with the reporting of the series, and I am happy to talk about the problems of the reporting issues, it is probably

12: JOHN WILLIAMS: THE COMING HYPER-INFLATION

the best quality broad economic statistic that the government publishes. Just don't pay too much attention to the month-to-month changes. It is much better than the GDP, and it is a coincident indicator of economic activity.

If you look at what has happened there, it plunged in late 2008 and 2009, and pretty much it has been bottom bouncing. It has moved a little bit higher, but it is far from having recovered the level that it was before the official recession started in 2007. I am talking about the level of payroll employment, the number of jobs that people are being paid for on company payrolls.

David: So, when we look at the employment statistics as they are issued, the U3 and U6 numbers, and of course, you do a reconfigured number there, which also factors in discouraged workers, short-term and long-term discouraged workers, what is our real picture? Are we closer to a 1973/1974 era of unemployment?

John: Yes, if you go back to the way the numbers used to be estimated, though it is impossible to fully reconstruct it, I think we are up around 22% unemployment. There have been problems going back over time, but you would find that it is probably about as bad as we have had since the great depression, which would take you back into the mid 1970s recession.

There is a very important point on the payrolls that I would just to get in here, and that is that the current level of payroll employment, the most recent reporting, is well below where it was in December of 2007 in the recession. It is also well below where it was at the beginning of the recession in 2001, ten years ago.

The payrolls today are below where they were a decade ago, and that is despite a 10% growth in the population. There is no way you can look at that and think of it being a normal economic circumstance. It's not there, it's an absolute catastrophe. There are all sorts of game-playing and hyping by Wall Street and the politicians, but we are going through a major structural change.

It has a long way to play out, and looking at the issues that we were discussing very briefly in terms of the deficit and the spending, a lot of the forecasts, going forward, on the federal budget deficit, for example, are based on assumptions of underlying economic growth. We are not going to have that, so the deficit is going to be a lot worse, the funding needs of the Treasury are going to be a lot worse, and all this combines together in, really, a perfect storm for the financial markets.

David: What you have just said is precisely what we see real-time in Greece. It was just a few months ago that they had resolved the Greek debt issue, they had a 50% haircut, which was done on a "voluntary basis," and now they are finding that growth in the economy, that was one of the assumptions that you just said we have, as well, was not as robust as needed, as expected, as factored in, and 50% is not going to be enough of a haircut. Maybe 60%, I've even heard numbers as high as 75%, and this is the issue.

They did buy themselves 3–4 months through the jawboning and through the exercise, but ultimately, nothing on a structural basis was changed. They didn't increase their revenues, they didn't decrease their expenses, and they still have a massive amount of debt as overhang, and that really does sound a lot like us. Although we are not Greece, our numbers and the circumstance we are in are similar.

John: Yes.

David: Too much debt overhang, revenue deficiency, and spending that is out of control.

John: The big difference is that Greece can no longer print drachmas. We can, and still do, print dollars. Within the European Union there are ways in which you can behave and you can't just issue, willy-nilly, a domestic currency when you no longer have a domestic currency. You get into the issue of the way the credit rating agencies look at this.

Normally, a credit rating agency would not give anything less than a Triple A rating to a sovereign debt issued in the currency of the sovereign. The rationale behind that is that the sovereign always has the ability to print the money to pay the debt, and the credit ratings are based on risk of default. On that basis, in theory, there should have been no downgrade to the US Treasuries.

The reason we had the downgrade was not because we have put ourselves in a position of long-term insolvency for the US government. Indeed, we have done that, but it was that with the debt ceiling in place, and the threats of default and the fighting over that, and the risk of default was no longer viewed as zero, in which a country could just print the money, but that you could actually have a formal default. That is why we had the downgrade in the US dollar.

But the US dollar is still a currency where we have been able to, and always can, at least as things are currently structured, print whatever money we need to meet our obligations. Greece does not have that opportunity. The situation in Europe is an unhappy one. I don't think the euro ever should have been put together.

The people who thought that Germany could align its fiscal policies with Greece and Italy and France just didn't know the countries involved. There was a strong desire among some to get a unified currency, but we are seeing that circumstance fall apart at this point in time.

In many ways, if you broke the euro into its constituent currencies, you would probably find the euro, recombined, would be a lot stronger than it is now. The markets are overly discounting the cost of Greece on the European system, but that will resolve itself. I am not a specialist on the euro circumstance, but I can tell you with virtual certainty, that if there is any event that currently is foreseeable, and there has certainly been enough time to work through all the different scenarios that may come from this, the Fed has been looking very carefully at what could bring about a domino effect in the system that could bring down the US banking system.

The Fed will do whatever it has to do to prevent the collapse of the banking system. If it has to bail out Italy, it will bail out Italy. Mr. Bernanke has the ability to do that. But the US Treasury doesn't, and the US Treasury right now is probably under some political constraints. But if we end up with the type of circumstance that we had following the Lehman collapse in 2008, I think even there we would find Congress moving to prevent a systemic collapse, that is, a failure of the banking system, and an absolute failure for the Fed.

It is not a circumstance anyone in Washington wants to see, but there is nothing they can do to fundamentally fix it. All they can do is kick the proverbial can down the road. I think we are going to have one more attempt here at kicking the can, but in doing so, we are also going to be collapsing the dollar, and that is going to accelerate the process toward hyperinflation.

David: You have picked a time frame of 2014–2018 and have begun to shrink that a bit more toward the 2014 horizon?

John: I put 2014 as an outside timing of this.

David: As an outside timing.

12: JOHN WILLIAMS: THE COMING HYPER-INFLATION

John: I would contend that we are actually through some of the early stages of it. Although we are not seeing the inflation, we have passed some of the benchmark things that have to happen for this to play out, and that, very specifically, is the global loss of confidence in the US dollar.

David: Let me focus on two things here, because, first of all, this is just repeating what I said earlier. If listeners aren't willing to invest a few dollars in the report at your subscription service, there are some things you need to do. I would suggest you order Adam Ferguson's book, *When Money Dies*. In this book you see the historical side of a hyperinflation. It is not so much the economic, but the social, political, and cultural changes that one experiences in that context, and I think that is worth knowing what it looks and feels like. How you get there, in terms of the economics—that's where you need to fast forward and look at this from 2004, or the 2014 or 2020 inevitability, which you just described, and now, all of a sudden those puzzle pieces being in place for it to be a present tense reality.

Again, if you are not going to go to ShadowStats.com and spend $89 for a six-month subscription, $175 for a one-year subscription, have this report and all of the other resources that come from shadowstats, what you are doing is limiting your ability to thrive and survive, in what is an absolute catastrophe.

Please do not trivialize the interview with John Williams today, because this is a look ahead at something that we would agree with John is a virtual certainty. The question is timing. We don't know when, but we certainly see this moving, and there is an acceleration that is taking place. As one of our guests from Europe has said, "Crisis compresses time," and things which have taken ten years to occur before are now happening within months, and within quarters, and will ultimately take place in weeks and days.

That is the nature of hyperinflation, as confidence is lost, and as there is a crisis, it is the psychological crisis, in which the telltales are in the currency, and you can see what is happening by the devaluation of the currency, but it is actually a psychological snap.

John: I can't argue with anything you just said there.

David: John, in light of this, we look at two things: First of all, we know that you can still go to ShadowStats.com and read the past copy, if you will, the special commentary #357, your Hyperinflation Special Report for 2011. Please take the time to read the 2012 version, as well, but the general public can go and read the 2011 version now. Maybe you can bring this into perspective. Sometimes we look at Germany as an instance of hyperinflation, but what about Zimbabwe? That is a little bit more present tense.

John: There are lessons from both, but one of the remarkable things about Zimbabwe is that it had probably the worst hyperinflation that any nation has ever experienced. Take the two-dollar bill from the original currency, and then go through all the iterations and lopping of zeros from the notes that they had over time, 100-trillion dollar notes. I don't think they went to a quadrillion because no one knew what a quadrillion was.

But if you were to come up with a two-dollar bill in the last version of the currency and make a pile of those that equaled the original two-dollar bill, that pile would have stretched from the earth to the Andromeda Galaxy, literally light years high. There are not enough trees on earth to print it, just absolute devastation in terms of the currency's value.

The hyperinflation, however, took place, and accelerated, over a period of a couple of years. At that same time, the economy still

12: JOHN WILLIAMS: THE COMING HYPER-INFLATION

functioned, although there were problems, and people worked, but the way they survived, the way the economy continued to function, was that they had a black market in US dollars. If you were paid in Zimbabwe dollars, you could immediately convert them into US dollars. You did that, and had a store of wealth, and you could operate off of that.

The problem in the United States is that we are dealing with the world's reserve currency, the largest economy. We have no such black market in the United States. We don't have a backup to the dollar, at least at this point in time. Without that, we would see a much more rapid and devastating impact on the economy. We would see disruption in supplies to grocery stores, food deliveries, and if we've got the food off the shelves in the grocery store, that's about as fast a way I can think of to start triggering civil disorder. It becomes a very dangerous situation.

What I am about to cover is not at all political. The gentleman, Dr. Ron Paul, who is running for the presidency on the Republican side of the primaries now, introduced legislation in Congress—at least the man is thinking—that would make gold legal tender, that it could be treated as a currency, so that you could take Federal Reserve Notes and exchange them for gold at the ongoing exchange rate without any tax consequence. If something like that actually were put into place, you would then have a functional backup for the dollar, for the Federal Reserve Notes, which are going to go through this hyperinflation.

That, in many ways, would mitigate some of the immediate devastation that you would see in the economy. It would actually be a plus for the economy, if something like that could be put into place, but I don't see that happening. I just mention it because this is something that has arisen in the last year and is new since I last updated the hyperinflation report.

David: It would certainly represent a challenge to the monopoly status of Federal Reserve notes and regarding all of those dear-hearted, wonderful Federal Reserve bankers, I don't know that they would be super-enthusiastic about that competition.

John: That's putting it mildly.

David: (Laughter) John, like books, there are ideas that need to be tasted, others chewed, and others yet digested, and here we are looking at inflation and the consequences, socially, politically—real decisions that have to be made in light of the things that are in the pipeline already. These are the things that we really need to ruminate on. Join us next week as we continue the conversation on these same issues and explore them further with you.

Kevin: David, what a fascinating interview so far. I can't wait to hear what is going to be said next week, but I think the thing that we have to focus on is that he is saying that hyperinflation is a "fait accompli." It is something that will occur, that the government has already pre-programmed into this economy. I think the thing that numbs us to hyperinflation is just how quickly it can hit. You can go from a state of almost zero inflation to a state of hyperinflation, such as in Germany, and ultimately, in Zimbabwe.

David: Kevin, I think there is a remarkable similarity with hyperinflation, that snap event that occurs, and what we see in the debts markets. Oftentimes, what you will see is perfect stability, and ideal pricing, interest rates at all-time lows, signifying that there is no risk in the system, just before you have a snap in interest rates, and all of a sudden you can go from a 2 to a 10, in terms of an interest rate. That is what we have seen in the debt panics all throughout Latin America. There is that interesting component where something changes, and it really is more of a psychological event than one that is even monetary.

12: JOHN WILLIAMS: THE COMING HYPER-INFLATION

Kevin: David, this reminds me of the tragedy that is occurring in Italy right now, with the cruise ship that sank. If you have ever been on a cruise ship, it is as if you are in another world. You don't really feel like you are on a boat at all. You can barely feel the rocking of the boat, you have all the food that you need, you have your room, you've got light, you've got entertainment, and what happened in Italy is, that just suddenly changed.

David: In fact, they thought that somebody was making good decisions for them, when in fact, the captain of the ship prioritized his own survival over the obligations that he had as "captain."

Kevin: He made bad decisions, and then he abandoned ship. I'm not saying that Ben Bernanke is going to abandon ship, but he sure is making bad decisions.

David: It does point us to one thing, Kevin. In the context of hyperinflation, and John, this is where we would like to take the conversation next week, it is in the direction of an individual understanding their responsibility and the choices that they have to make in order to do well, survive, and thrive, in a period of time of incredible stress and chaos, brought about by economic and financial mismanagement.

A few weeks later, John appeared again on the weekly "McAlvany Commentary," and again his message was clear: hyperinflation by 2014. This second interview took place on January 25, 2012, and is presented here in entirety.

MP3 Hyperlink: www.McalvanyWeeklyCommentary.com/wp-content/uploads//ica2012-0125.mp3

Kevin: David, last week we had John Williams on the program and of course, again, as promised, we have him on this week. The subject was hyperinflation, as much as we would like to avoid it.

David: There is the classic funny question and answer, "How did you go broke?" "Very slowly, and then all at once." That really captures the idea of hyperinflation, where it didn't appear on anyone's radar screen, and then all of a sudden it was the state of affairs. There was no gradual slippage. We saw that in Germany, going from 6% in 1918 to 100% in 1919, and then into the thousands of percents per year, a very rapid acceleration.

One thing we want to talk about, John, as we enter the conversation today, is the velocity of money, being either an indication of a return to economic health as it picks up, or as people are dumping their currency and it spins out of control and the velocity ends up being a multiple of what anyone could expect it to be.

John, this last year, on our film, one of the things that we talked about was the importance of the velocity of money. Essentially, velocity is flat, the transmission mechanism. The central banks can print, and they have created a tremendous amount of liquidity, but what we find is that excess reserves are being held with the Fed.

There is not a lot of circulation of liquidity, printed liquidity, provided into the larger economy. You might see velocity pick up if the economy was picking up, but you could also see velocity spin out of control and rapidly ramp up in a hyperinflation. How would you suggest we view velocity? Conceptually, how would it be a helpful tool for us to anticipate entering the next round of inflation, super, or even hyperinflation?

John: Conceptually, velocity is very important. Velocity—the number of times that the money supply turns over in the econo-

12: JOHN WILLIAMS: THE COMING HYPER-INFLATION

my—is part of the basic formula that relates economic and inflation activity to the growth in the money supply. It is very difficult to measure because, as a residual, the GNP numbers are worthless, the GDP numbers are worthless. They are not heavily modeled, as I mentioned earlier, just to take a look at what is happening with payroll, the number is an indication of relative economic activity.

The GDP, as it gets reported, is net of inflation, but the inflation numbers are underestimated, deliberately. The methodologies have been changed to reduce reported inflation. If inflation were accurately reported, the inflation-adjusted GDP would have shown a deeper decline and absolutely no recovery, and the official GDP right now actually is higher than it was before the economy turned down.

But it is challenging to find any other economic statistics that show that pattern. It hasn't happened. It is all in the gimmick-weighted GDP reporting. So you divide that by the money supply and the best the government does right now is report M2. I still follow the old M3, which was, at the time, the broader measure. They used to report an L measure, including private holdings of treasury bills. They chose not to continue reporting on that, but even with the M3, there are issues in terms of what is being measured, and when you are dealing with the world's reserve currency, you also have to consider the money supply that is sitting outside the system, sitting outside the United States.

Whereas M3 right now is maybe around 14 trillion dollars, there is at least a 7-trillion dollar overhang of dollars that can be dumped into our system, and you have to consider that a little bit in terms of how it works into the overall velocity picture. Basically, what you are talking about is a basic number. The faster the velocity turns over, people don't want to hold the dollars. That becomes a key element of the hyperinflation, and again, we may already be seeing that.

Consider that, within the traditional spectrum of investment sold by Wall Street, there is no safe investment out there in which an investor can put his money and beat inflation, even as reported by the US government. In that type of a circumstance, you would do better to take your cash and go out and buy the consumer goods that are inflating, because at least you will keep up with inflation that way, and you would be ahead of what you would get on a Treasury bill. And people are beginning to see a little bit of that. That tends to spike the velocity.

Again, there is no easy way to measure it. It is a matter of having to look at it anecdotally as to whether or not it is picking up, but there will be a rapid pickup here again as we see the panic decline globally, dumping of the dollars. No one wants to hold the dollars. You will see that beginning in the US, as well. As that pace accelerates, the velocity will be a major factor driving the prices higher.

David: You are talking about not only M3, but the international supply of US dollars, which the 14 trillion plus the 7 trillion—$21 trillion total—would be a basic footprint for greenbacks. Now, of course, you are talking about a multiple of that, depending on how fast it goes through the economy. 21 x 2, 21 x 3, 21 x 5—however many times that $21 trillion is being circulated—that is, in fact, what can be deceptive at the front edge of a hyperinflation. Because with that increase in transactions, if you will, we are seeing business return to "normal," but it is not actually normal. It is like the surfer who thinks he has the perfect wave, not realizing it is a tsunami. He's going to enjoy it.

John: It isn't even necessarily returning to normal. There is an important point, here, in terms of inflation. There are a couple of kinds of inflation, the way consumers see it. The healthy kind is when you do have a strong economy and people have money, and they are out spending, and there is more money chasing too few goods. That is a relatively happy circumstance—production increases—those are good economic times, even though you may have higher inflation.

Then you have the not-so-happy inflation, which is what Mr. Bernanke has been creating, and again, we have to go back to 2002 when the Fed chairman got his nickname of Helicopter Ben, he made a speech on how the Fed could always prevent a deflation. There was a fear of deflation. The fear is of the type of deflation that was seen during the Great Depression where prices dropped maybe a third, in aggregate. That reflected the contraction in the money supply. The money supply contracted a third.

The reason they had that terrible deflation, although people argue that deflation has positive elements to it, as well, I am not getting into the merits of deflation or inflation here, but just how it works mechanically. The reason we had that sharp decline in prices was because of the collapse in the banking system, and with the number of people having cash in the banks actually losing their deposits. They no longer had the money they thought they had, that they had had on deposit with the bank that failed.

In the current era where we have the FDIC and the Fed steps in or the Treasury steps in, in a crisis such as we had in 2008, and pretty much guarantees everything there, then the people holding cash in banks are covered. But as they lost the cash, that created the collapse in the money supply. The debt crisis didn't crash the money supply, so it was a little different. The bank lends a million dollars, you spend that in the system, it goes all over the place, and, in theory, if the system is operating normally, which we have not seen in some years, that million dollars will end up as 10 million dollars of money supply.

Then you default on your loan to the bank, the bank comes to you and says, "Give me back the million dollars," and you say, "I'm sorry, I can't do it." The bank can't go into the system and pull out of the system that million dollars, or the 10 million dollars, and the money supply that million dollars created. So it doesn't contract the money supply. What it does, though, is hurt the balance sheet of the bank, and as the bank's balance sheet takes a hit, its ability to lend is reduced.

That is part of the reason behind the lack of growth in bank lending that we are still seeing—very, very weak. That is the reason we are not seeing the growth in bank lending, because the banks are not stable, they are not long-term solvent, or the system isn't. So they are not lending the money, and they've slowed the money supply, but now the money supply is growing and I can tell you that of the last numbers that we have tracked, three were at the highest level in something like 28 months, and the most recent numbers are suggesting it is beginning to spike a little bit.

David: There are concerns, domestically, and you mentioned that. Something as basic as food delivery and what can happen on the basis of that, causing civil disorder in the event of a super or hyper-inflation. We also live in a world where the US dollar is the reserve currency and there are over 50 countries that are dollarized, that actually use the US dollar. What are the geopolitical implications for these dollarized countries, and for our foreign relationships, as we move toward a hyperinflationary end game?

John: It is not going to be very good for those countries that are dollarized or those that try to peg to the dollar. They will be suffering the same type of debasement in the currency that we will be seeing here. We will see all sorts of effects. There is some moaning and groaning in China about importing inflation from US monetary policy, but that's because they are still pegging their currency to the dollar, to a certain extent, and as the dollar sinks, and this is where the inflation comes in, I sort of got distracted from that, but as the dollar declines, and we have plenty of dollar-selling ahead of us.

Right now we are seeing an artificial propping of the currency, but, as the dollar declines, we have commodities such as oil that are denominated in dollars, and the way that the effect works through in the markets is that the dollar decline will tend to spike prices in dollar terms. That becomes inflationary. To us, the inflation that we have seen in the United States over the last year, the pickup there, we are still up nearly 3½%, year over year, it has a long way to go to the upside, but that is not because of any underlying strength in the economy. It is largely due to higher gasoline prices, which are not due to strong demand, it is due to the dollar distortion and the spike in oil prices.

The higher oil prices also are working their way into the broad economy. I can't think of any commodity more important than oil in terms of its impact on consumer inflation. Any goods that get transported, driving energy, the pharmaceutical industries, a lot of materials based on that, chemical industry, fertilizers, plastics—all that is tied to the price of oil.

Bernanke likes to push the concept of core inflation, which is the inflation measure, net of inflation, including energy. Absolute nonsense to look at that on a long-term basis, because those are two of the most important components of consumption for individuals. If you look at it on a monthly basis and say, "Oh yeah, there was a big jump this month," but that is because oil prices were up, or food prices were up.

That's a legitimate consideration, but when you look at it on a year-over-year basis, you are no longer looking at short-term distortions, and guess what? If you look at the core CPI, as published by the government, it started turning up when Mr. Bernanke started to jawbone the dollar lower before QE-II, and it has risen every month, year over year, since then.

And we are likely going to see another jump of that in the month of December, which, as we are talking, is just ahead of us. It is spreading throughout the economy. This next round of inflation or weakness in the dollar will be much more severe in terms of its effect on commodities and plus, people have to go to work. They are going to buy gasoline. They may not go for leisurely drives in the country, but it is going to be cutting into their available income, and they are going to turn all the cash they have over faster and faster to just try to stay even, let alone gain, in what people would hope for as a healthy economy. But we are not going to have a healthy economy, as we go into this.

David: Let me ask you just to peg a probability. As we look at 2012 and see that there has been very little political will to address the circumstances that we are in, from a fiscal and economic standpoint, what do you think the probabilities are of our government leaders, and the folks, both between Washington and New York, kicking the can down the road, specifically into 2013, past the election? Can we see them buy time for 12 months, or is the probability too great of seeing this domino effect from Europe?

John: Well, they would certainly like to kick the can that far down the road. I will contend they can't. They will try, but in order to be able to do that, they still have to get people to buy the Treasury funding needs, which they are having trouble doing, to wit, the Fed has done all that the last year. And they find that the Fed has to come in and become the lender of last resort to the US government. The hyperinflation follows very quickly with that, and along with that, the rest of the world is dumping the dollar.

12: JOHN WILLIAMS: THE COMING HYPER-INFLATION

What is distorting the dollar right now is the distraction of the problems in Europe. That will pass, and the Federal Reserve, the US players in this will do whatever is necessary to protect the US banking system from collapse. But as the European situation eases back the markets will begin to say, "Gee, what's going on here?" And the elephant in the bathtub is the dollar, and people have been missing that.

They started to see it in August, and then we could have been off to the races at that point in time, but again, we can expect that there will be interventions, sleight of hand, all sorts of things that will come into play, but it doesn't change the underlying fundamentals. They don't have until 2015 to keep the markets at bay. The global markets will turn on the dollar, and they are very close to doing so.

If you are OPEC—and this is where the dollarized countries come in, too—the dollar is going to be debased, and that is the policy of the Fed. That is what Mr. Bernanke wanted to do. We can always prevent deflation, which is the fear of what we had in the 1930s and the effects of the banking system collapse. We can always, with the central bank working in concert with the sovereign power—they can always debase their currency, create inflation. They can. It's easy for them to create inflation or to knock the economy down. The negatives are easy to do.

What is very tough to do is to contain the inflation and to stimulate the economy, but they can't do either of those at the moment. The actions that it takes are aimed at maintaining banking system solvency, and all of the talk about stimulating the economy is just fluff for popular consumption and acceptance of the policies.

David: We've seen the Saudi Oil Minister raise the expected oil price from $75 a barrel to $100 a barrel just this week. I think it was in 2008 that they contended $75 was sufficient and that is what they would target. Now they say $100 is sufficient and that is what they will target. I think you are right. What we are seeing from the 2008 to 2011 period is an adjustment, if you will, an accommodation, of lower dollar values and dollar instability, anticipating that into the future, reflecting on a per barrel basis.

Let me ask you a quick question on our domestic politics and then we will wrap up. We are in an election year. We should see some statistics absolutely tortured to sing the song that they are supposed to, whether it is for the incumbent or not, and we are interested in—if this is 2013, 2014—an era of hyperinflation. We are talking about the political party that wins; it will probably be anathema for the next 10, 20, 30 years. It really isn't a time to go out and pursue victory, is it?

John: This could break before the election. We have all sorts of unusual things at play here. Over the last century, generally, the presidential elections were very predictable, given income growth, net of inflation. And, at least in the way it used to be measured, whenever disposable income, the take-home pay, of the average individual, was above 3.2%, the incumbent party retained the White House, and when it was below 3.2% of income, the incumbent party lost the White House, and that worked consistently over time.

We are seeing no growth in disposable income now, net of inflation. This is the type of environment that, with two parties, Mr. Obama would be facing forced retirement at the end of the year in 2012, just due to the economy. The economy hurt George Bush. That's one reason that Obama was elected. But what we are seeing here is so severe, and so painful, that it can bring about unusual change—enough so that the establishment guys may have some surprises, and I say the establishment guys—

12: JOHN WILLIAMS: THE COMING HYPER-INFLATION

governments are corrupt. They have been as far back as governments have existed.

As long as people are doing well, the average person doesn't seem to care too much. But once they start feeling economic pain, they tend to look very closely at the people running the circumstance, and that is when the guys that have been having a great time run into some trouble. This is the type of environment in which if there is no real change offered by either major party that you could have a third party come to the fore, and maybe knock either the Republicans or the Democrats into third party status.

My betting is that we are probably not going to see a change in the establishment kind of president in this election which will, again, just accelerate and doom the process for hyperinflation. If you had someone who could, today, go in and actually argue for the change and make changes and talk honestly to the American people and say, "Hey look, we're bankrupt. This has been a problem with both parties over the years. We have gone beyond our means and if we don't bring it under control now, our style of life, and our financial world, as we know it, is not going to survive. We have to make painful cuts that are going to affect almost everyone in these circumstances." Then the American people could understand and rally around. They already sense there is a problem.

If that is not addressed by the major parties, we are going to have a third party. I don't know if it is going to be powerful enough to make the change, but if we can get a real shift so that instead of lacking the political will to address the system, we have the political will to overhaul it, maybe there is something that can be done to enforce the law. I don't see it happening, but it would be good if it could.

THE COMING BANKING HOLIDAY

I think I mentioned this with you the last time we talked. I have only been physically assaulted once for my views, and that was by a very nice elderly lady at a bank board meeting in Maine. She broke into tears and said, "All you have here is bad news. Where is the good news?" She was so upset she took a jelly donut and threw it at me and hit me right in the middle of the chest. She had a very good arm. Before I could say anything, the bank chairman stepped in and he said, "The good news is, you know it's happening, and if you know it's happening, you can protect yourself."

If I saw a way the government could actually resolve this, if I thought there was a chance of it, I would be out pushing that real hard. I don't see it happening. There's a chance, but if I had to put the odds on it, it's not going to happen, which means I'm out talking about how you can protect yourself. That's what the individual has to look at. The system, I think, has gone too far to right itself within the day-to-day politics that we have seen for the last 30–40 years. It will become self-righting as the system gets into this terrible financial turmoil.

Individuals, hopefully, will be able to ride out the storm, and they can do that by looking to preserve their wealth and assets and look at physical gold, such as sovereign coins, as a primary hedge, getting some assets outside the US dollar. It is going to be primarily a US dollar problem, getting into stronger currencies. When you look at the artificial intervention, those things don't last, and usually provide an opportunity for people who are betting against the intervention.

If you can protect your assets, keep them liquid, you will ride out the storm. Then you are in a position to not only have survived, but you will be in a position to make some very unusual investments after the fact, or you will be happy that you were able to maintain your assets and liquidity. If we don't get something like the Ron Paul bill, which gives you backup to the dollar, and again, my betting is that you are not going to see anything there.

You also need to look at personal safety. If the grocery store shelves get cleaned out, you should have a stock of canned food, like you might for a natural disaster. I'm crazy enough to be sitting here on the Hayward fault in California. I didn't come out here to sit on the Hayward fault, I came out here to be close to family, and we discussed these issues, but I am, nonetheless, here, and beyond whatever I am looking at from the financial standpoint, I do have a stock of goods that would see me through an earthquake.

You should look at disasters that could hit you and where you need to be prepared and have a basic store of goods that will get you through a couple of months before a barter system would kick in, for example. Do that for a man-made disaster, as well as a natural disaster. Use stuff that you can circulate and turn the inventories over. There is very little cost to that. And in fact, in an inflationary environment, in which we are now, when you look at consumer goods against what you can get in the way of return on a T-bill, you are actually saving money.

David: John, we appreciate you joining us again, and we will certainly want to have this conversation again before we get to that outside date of 2014. There is a story to be told within the statistics that you look at, and we want our clients and listeners to be well advised ahead of time, to make the requisite choices, the needed choices, so that they are not surprised and held captive by being on the wrong side of things, forced to play the patience game and wait it out.

We, again, look forward to the future conversation and appreciate your contribution. Shadowstats.com is where our listeners can go and download the Hyperinflation Special Report. Looking at last year's is of great value, and we would also encourage you to subscribe to the service and look at the update. That will be out in the next few days.

John, thanks again for joining us.

John: Thank you so much for having me.

Kevin: David, I think the summary of what John was saying is, in a way, a little bit spooky. He is talking about hyperinflation, but he also has made a very clear point, both last week and this week, that this is probably unsolvable with any political solution.

David: Kevin, there are political solutions, but they are not on offer, and that is what I think we are missing in terms of the stock of folks who are coming into the election cycle this time around. We would have to go back to the Harding administration. We would have to consider cutting the budget by 50%. We would have to take dramatic action to see a major fix on the fiscal side of things, and that is why we see this correction as primarily a correction via the currency. And we translate hyperinflation, or super inflation, as correcting the financial excesses of the last 20–30 years via an adjustment in the currency to a much lower value.

Kevin: Honestly, David, this show is not really trying to correct the country's problem, or the world's problems. We are too small for that. But what we can do is to talk to each listener and say exactly what John Williams said, and that is, if it can't be solved politically, and it may not be able to be solved economically on the large scale, you have to protect yourself. You have to preserve your assets, and not just survive, but maybe thrive, maybe be able to have pennies on the dollar types of buys on the other side of this tunnel.

David: I think having an open mind, Kevin, and being willing to take certain actions now, just makes sense. As he said, it is very common sense when you live in California to prepare for an earthquake, because these things do happen. Yet, you live your day, hoping for the best, prepared for the worst, and being ready for anything. That is, I think the way we need to enter 2012 and 2013.

Courtesy of the McAlvany Weekly Commentary with David McAlvany and Kevin Orrick

Our comment: John Williams from Shadowstats is one of the last of the honest, factual statisticians following the numbers coming out of Washington. His calculations of real unemployment at 22% and real inflation at about 11% are alarming, and dwarf the stats coming out of today's administration. Hyper-inflation hitting no later than 2014? That's pretty scary stuff, and it is hoped that those reading this book will take action way prior to this date.

A side note to thank David McAlvany for the use of this incredible interview: I started on Wall Street with his father, Don McAlvany, in 1967 (at the investment firm of Hayden Stone, Inc.). David appears to be following nicely in his father's footprints, and I wish he, and his staff, much success.

Our action: We have been planning for hyper-inflation since 2005 when we left the US. We exited the general stock market that year, sold all our real estate holdings that year, and placed the proceeds into gold in Switzerland (Credit Suisse). For barter purposes, we purchased silver coins (stored in an Auckland depository).

CHAPTER THIRTEEN

Don't Put All Your Eggs (Assets) in One Country

"History shows us that when governments decline and fail, they cannibalize the citizenry and shake every last nickel they can from the sheeple. It doesn't matter who you are—a retired schoolteacher, a small business owner, a struggling single mother—everyone becomes a target.

Everyone ultimately has a choice. We can either choose to be a target and be safely diversified abroad, or we can choose to be a target and have all of our assets in one basket for easy pickings. We'll all be targets regardless."

—Simon Black, SovereignMan.com

The greatest risk we all face is sovereign risk—having everything in a single country (i.e., holding all your eggs in a single sovereign basket).

Simply put, if you live, work, own property, store gold, bank, invest, structure a business, hold retirement funds, etc. in a single country, then all your assets and interests are at great risk when something happens in that country.

And the list of things that could go wrong is long:

Your assets can be frozen or seized at the whim of any judge, bureaucrat, or police agency, and you are guilty until proven innocent. Politicians routinely change laws effective immediately (or, even worse, retroactively) meaning capital gains taxes and income taxes can rise dramatically overnight, or *new* taxes can be imposed. Considering the alarming rate at which local, state, and federal governments are going broke, these threats become more realistic every day and in fact are already happening.

Capital controls and currency debasement are also major issues. Desperate governments have historically tried to control their money supplies by restricting the free flow of capital across borders, preventing businesses and citizens from moving money out of the country, holding it captive to inflationary policies, senseless regulation, and higher taxes.

Sovereign Risk threatens everyone's livelihood, and not diversifying this risk is putting all of your eggs in one very frail little sovereign basket. Your livelihood depends on being able to properly diversify this risk. For those who are well prepared, this is a time not of fear, but of once in a century opportunity.

During this rough period, the die shall be cast for generations. Fortunately, we can clearly see this coming and there is still a bit of time to act...but diversifying Sovereign Risk requires a NEW, more global principle of diversification.

The NEW Global Principle of Diversification

The old, well-known "Principle of Diversification" says to avoid putting all your eggs in one basket. By diversifying your assets and putting them in different "baskets" you significantly reduce the risk of losing everything. It makes a lot of sense.

The old principle of diversification is commonly applied to financial assets. You put some money in stocks, bonds, real estate, maybe even precious metals like gold and silver.

The greatest risk we face in today's world is Sovereign Risk—the risk of holding all your eggs in a single sovereign basket—leaving everything to the whims of a single government.

THE COMING BANKING HOLIDAY

You could even diversify within those categories. Large-cap stocks, small-cap stocks, etc. As one class of assets fell in value, another would rise to offset it.

That principle served us well for several generations while the US prospered and became the world's dominant super power… but those days are quickly coming to an end (some argue those days are already in the rear view mirror). In any event, the US is not the world super power it once was.

In the short span of a few decades the United States has undergone a radical transformation in terms of its economic activity and behavior. The US became a super power by saving, producing, creating wealth, and exporting manufactured goods for the rest of the world to consume. Unfortunately, we have turned that upside down.

We have become a nation of non-savers, shifted from manufacturing to a largely non-exportable service-based economy, and run up record amounts of national and personal debt. We've mortgaged ourselves to the hilt and squandered the money largely on excessive consumption of unproductive imported goods. What we have done is similar to a philandering playboy who inherits a huge fortune and then proceeds to squander it.…

You understand the direction the world is heading. Without question, the pressure is building and the endgame cannot be far off.

Here's a prediction for you:

By this time next year, once people realize that the political process is a total fraud, there will be protests in cities throughout the world of such scale and anger that today's "Occupy" movement will look like a high school pep rally.

13: DON'T PUT ALL YOUR EGGS (ASSETS) IN ONE COUNTRY

Mass protests and angry rioting will give way to violence...and violence will be met with even greater violence from the state. Most people don't want to believe it. It could never happen here. We're different.

Dozens of societies throughout history thought the exact same thing. And yet, the proverbial stuff hits the fan. It's going to happen in our modern society too...and you're not going to want to be anywhere near it.

Fortunately, you still have time to act. The single biggest thing you can do to ensure the safety and security of the ones you love is to cover your downside risk. This includes things like:

1. Preserving your savings offshore in a strong, stable, international banking center.

2. Holding precious metals overseas.

3. Establishing a "bolt-hole" in a place far away from the anger, crime, and police state crackdowns.

Courtesy of Simon Black, Sovereign Man

THE COMING BANKING HOLIDAY

Our comment: It appears that Simon Black has summarized the entire book with this abbreviated essay. It makes sense, for those remaining in the US, to diversify their assets, and to do so in different parts of the world (for example, your savings account in NZ using Australian currency account, paying 4¼% interest, your gold in a Suisse depository, and your stocks in a custodian investment account in NZ. And let's not forget your silver coins, buried under their old oak tree).

Our action: We followed our own advice, except for silver. We don't have an old oak tree, as we are renting. Therefore, our silver is stored in an Auckland depository, 35 minutes away by ferry.

CHAPTER FOURTEEN

The "Urgency"

"What's happening in Washington now is destroying the class of people who save and invest. Think of all the people who saved their money over the past twenty years, put their money in the bank expecting to live off the interest in their retirement.... They are getting wiped out."

—*Jim Rogers*

Simon Black, like Porter Stansberry, definitely tells it as it really is. I read his daily commentaries and am continually amazed at his knowledge of world events. His publication, "Sovereign Man," is highly recommended. Monica and I wrote this book to tell you what we found out overseas, and this chapter tells you of the urgency to get your money and investments overseas. There are other places besides NZ and Australia to consider. We have done our homework and found these two countries perfect to safeguard our nest egg. Here are Simon's thoughts. You can feel the "urgency" in his essay.

All of these events are underpinned by a simple premise:

1. Public and private debts included, *most Western nations are insolvent.* Big time.

2. History shows that *economic growth in such an environment is nearly impossible* when such a large percentage of GDP must be allocated solely to interest. Most countries in this position either default or [hyper-]inflate. Both have catastrophic consequences.

3. *Continued political and monetary intervention in the economy is counterproductive.* From "Cash for Clunkers" to negative real interest rates, such intervention only serves to make the problems, and their impacts, much worse.

4. The combined ingredients of sovereign insolvency; a global financial system based on worthless paper currency; and consumptive, import-oriented, public entitlement economies have created *conditions for an epic, long-term economic depression.*

5. Deteriorating *economic conditions drive social unrest.* [In fact, there's a great paper by two European economists that

defines an explicit correlation between government budget cuts and things like rising crime rates, riots, and even attempted revolution.]

6. Faced with a marauding population that threatens their own survival, *governments will stop at nothing to maintain the status quo: their power, our expense.* Again, history shows that police states, boogeyman enemies, a total loss of privacy, capital controls, higher taxes, etc. will all become the norm.

7. None of these delay tactics can prevent human and financial capital from eventually migrating to where they are treated best. This will ultimately *force a complete system reset by starving the beast.*

8. *This is not the first time this has happened, and it won't be the last.* This time is NOT different. Our modern society is not a unique and special snowflake that can ward off the consequences that have plagued empires for millennia.

Everything from the way I invest to how I allocate my time and plan for the future is based on this view. It's why I'm in Chile, why we purchased a 1,000+ acre farm, and why we plan on sharing it with like-minded people.

I may be a bit early, but I'd much rather be early than thinking through these implications while I'm packing my bags. After all, things can "feel" quite normal for a long time. *Changes take place gradually, then faster and faster, until the decay looks like an upside-down hockey stick.*

The Roman Empire, for example, began its spectacular decline shortly after Augustus became de facto emperor in 27 BC. He was followed by a long series of dismal failures—Tiberius, Caligula, Claudius, Nero, etc. But Rome muddled along for hundreds of years, wavering between growth and decay.

The changes were gradual. A little currency debasement here, a bit of excess spending there, and throw in plenty of assassinations and foreign wars for good measure. Along the way, though, thinking people could see the writing on the wall... and many of Rome's citizens set sail for greener pastures.

The gradual changes became more and more pronounced... and the more pronounced, the more people left. As Gibbon recounts in his seminal work, The History of the Decline and Fall of the Roman Empire, *the city of Rome lost nearly 75% of its population in the Empire's final 50-years in the 5th century.*

History is full of other examples of once proud nations that, facing problems for decades (or even centuries), completely unwound in a matter of years. *The Ottoman Empire. The Ming Dynasty. Feudal France. The Soviet Union.*

Bottom line, *when the real change comes, it comes very, very quickly.*

Think about the pace of change these days. It's quickening. Europe is a great case study for this—when concerns about Greece first surfaced, European leaders were able to contain the damage. There was disquiet, but it soon dissipated.

Fast forward to today. We can hardly go a single day without a major, market-rocking headline. And European politicians' attempts to assuage the damage have a useful half-life that can be measured in days... sometimes hours now.

Like the Ottomans, the Soviets, the Romans before them, *Western civilization is entering the phase where its rate of decline will start looking like that upside-down hockey stick.*

14: THE "URGENCY"

There is no crystal ball that can tell us exactly how/when it will all go down. It stands to reason that certain events (perhaps this year's Presidential elections in the US, Russia, France, etc.) will be pivotal in the decline, but suffice it to say that *time is not on our side given the pace of change.*

Each of us has a finite amount of resources—time, energy, capital, etc. And I really want to encourage you to think clearly and deliberately about how you allocate those resources... e.g. you're better off buying an ounce of gold than making a political campaign contribution.

2011 was a challenging year. 2012 will likely prove even more. But this isn't anything to dread. *It's is an incredibly exciting time to be alive—change should be embraced, not feared.*

Empires always run their course. Bubbles burst. But creative, thinking human beings always survive and thrive.

Courtesy of Simon Black, Sovereign Man

THE COMING BANKING HOLIDAY

Our comment: As Simon says above: "When the real change comes, it comes very, very quickly." He isn't kidding. When we left in late 2005, all appeared just fine. The stock market was recovering, real estate was at an all-time high, and employment was rising. Looking back, just seven years later, the world is upside down, both financially and politically and, the process is accelerating.

Our action: We left for greener pastures, but still follow what's happening in America via the Internet. My job as a financial adviser in the US and NZ gets me up most mornings at 2 a.m. From that time until 10 a.m., I review my accounts, keeping them in *the strongest natural resource companies*. Life is good here on Waiheke Island, 35 minutes by ferry from Auckland.

CHAPTER FIFTEEN

The Crash of 2012

"When people lose everything and they have nothing left to lose, they lose it."

—Gerald Celente, *Trends Journal*

THE COMING BANKING HOLIDAY

In high school history class, the Great Depression was explained. We were taught, essentially, that in 1929 there was a stock market crash, and after that, lots of people were desperately poor. While this is true, the explanation is overly simplified to the point that there is no practical lesson we can learn from it.

Here's what actually happened: In the autumn of 1929, the first in a series of waves occurred in the stock market—a downward wave. It was followed by a rally (upward wave), then a much deeper and longer downward wave. This third wave, in turn, was followed by a series of smaller upward and downward waves until the market hit bottom in 1932–33.

In studying these waves (Elliott Wave Theory), it becomes apparent that the same waves occur in any major market fluctuation, and the degree of downside is always relative to the degree of upside. The third wave is always the most extreme.

Jeff Thomas, writing for International Man, anticipates that the third wave in the present series is imminent. It will be deeper and longer than the downward wave of 2008. The others will be smaller, but ultimately, together they will be more severe than the series of fluctuations from 1929 to 1932.

On the surface, it seems unlikely that financial downturns would behave predictably, but Elliott Wave Theory is based upon human nature. In any era, the reactions to events will be similar, as human nature remains the same, regardless of the era we live in. The present *unraveling* of the American Empire is remarkably similar to that of the Roman Empire and other empires in the interim.

15: THE CRASH OF 2012

A Little History

In 1933, the *Glass-Steagall Act* was passed in Congress. Its purpose was to create banking reforms to control speculation by banks, a root cause of the Great Depression. Ever since that time, economists and Congressmen alike have said, "Depressions are no longer a concern. There can be no more depressions." They stuck to that position, while forgetting that the control of possible depressions was directly linked to the continued existence of Glass-Steagall.

Beginning in the 1980s, the major banks began work to eliminate the Glass-Steagall Act in order to recreate the opportunity for enormous profit, similar to what occurred in the late 1920s. Although their efforts met with resistance, then Chairman of the Federal Reserve Alan Greenspan helped to convince the government of the day to vote in favor of the repeal. The premise was that America was positioned to create a housing boom of historic proportions, making possible home ownership for millions of people who previously would not have qualified for a loan. It was further suggested that banks could not fulfill this opportunity without the repeal of Glass-Steagall.

Conservative Congressmen saw the benefits to both commerce and the banking industry in this concept. Liberal Congressmen saw the hope for millions of average people to have homes. Glass-Steagall was repealed with everyone's blessing.

Unfortunately, few, if any, of those Congressmen who voted for this repeal bothered to learn why Glass-Steagall had been drafted in the first place, and the stage was now set for the Greater Depression.

Small minorities of prognosticators have been harping on the prediction of a "Greater Depression" since the late 1990s. We anticipated that a housing bubble would develop, followed by a massive crash, and that the stock market would then also begin its crash. Thomas believed that the warning sign that this was on the verge of occurring would be that "Teflon Alan" would resign as Chairman of the Fed at least one year prior to the disaster, as he would want to distance himself from it. This he did in 2006, leaving Ben Bernanke to hold the bag.

Thomas also predicted that the crash would not come all at once; that, as always in history, it would be a series of waves. However, the majority of people would follow what they had been told by their high school history books. As soon as there was a rally of significant proportions (second wave), they would believe that recovery had arrived. They would believe this in spite of the fact that the massive debt still existed and, like a cancer, still required elimination before real prosperity could follow.

If we are correct, and the Greater Depression is in its first stages, the worst (by far) is yet to come.

What Goes Up Must Come Down

When a small bull market crashes, the crash is small. When a large bull market crashes, the crash is big. This concept is a simple one that anyone will accept. So, what happens when the largest bull market in over 300 years crashes?

And if the current rally, presently being described as a recovery, were to behave like the 1929–1930 upward wave, when would it end? When would we know that it is not a recovery, and is just a rally similar to the 1930 rally?

The answer, in my belief, is very soon.

15: THE CRASH OF 2012

The third wave in the collapse could have occurred as early as mid-2010, but the economy was artificially propped up by Quantitative Easing (QE). This type of action can postpone the eventual third wave, but not eliminate it. In fact, postponement only assures a deeper drop when the third wave does occur.

With the ending of QE2, many have been holding their breath to see what will happen next. They will not have to wait long, and the fall off the mountain will be directly proportional to the climb up the mountain. The market peak is imminent, and, based on Elliott Wave Theory, the subsequent fall (should it begin soon) may take six years, ending in 2018.

Why, Historically, a Large Collapse Is Likely

Very few people who are alive today were around in 1929, so, understandably, the very concept of such a debacle seems like the work of overly-active and overly-pessimistic minds. For that reason, a further examination is needed as to what has led up to this occurrence.

1. The mania up until 2008 was the biggest since the 1720–1784 mania. It should therefore result in a deeper decline than in 1929–1933.

2. Declines following manias always carry below the starting point of the mania. The crashes following the Tulip Mania of the 1630s, the South Sea Bubble of the early 1700s and the Roaring Twenties bull market, all brought prices to below the level of the bull markets' starting points. In this case, the mania-style bull market started in 1974.

3. Thanks to the great rise in positive social mood during our present mania, the stock market remains historically over-

valued in terms of dividends and earnings. (When people without jobs are provided with loans to buy multiple houses, with no money down, it becomes reasonable to believe that pigs have wings.)

4. The greatest extreme in positive social mood in centuries has led to the greatest expansion of credit in history. This level of outstanding debt is unsustainable and will be unserviceable and unpayable. The trend toward negative social mood that has begun, and which is about to accelerate, will continue to curtail lending, leading to a tidal wave of defaults and a major deflation in equities.

5. The trend toward negative social mood, concurrent with a collapse of the market, will lead to an economic contraction. Small bear markets lead to recessions; big bear markets lead to depressions. The recent mania was the biggest in nearly 300 years, so the depression will be correspondingly deep.

6. As a by-product, this trend of major negative social mood will bring a frightening degree of social unrest. Under such conditions, people who, for years, had seen only increases in entitlements and suddenly find those entitlements disappearing will not accept diminished entitlements quietly. If they do not receive what they had been promised, many will choose to take what they want from whomever they can. An inkling into this trend can presently be viewed by us from afar by examining a similar, more minor situation playing out in the streets of Europe.

7. People will desire what they consider to be money, not stocks. A concurrent gold mania will occur. Gold, silver and other traditional, dependable commodities will become the basis of wealth, and fiat currency will decline in value dramatically.

15: THE CRASH OF 2012

This outlook is extreme and is difficult even to imagine. As mentioned previously, no one alive has ever seen anything like it, and it is understandable for us to say to ourselves, "It can't possibly be that bad. At worst, we might have a double-dip recession, but we'll get past it." However, all of the above is based upon historical occurrences and consistent patterns.

It will be a ragged decline. The banking system will not deteriorate all at once; the crisis will occur piecemeal, with some events more devastating than others. Some communities will be harder hit than others. Those who are more independent of commerce (ranchers, small farmers) will not be as affected, as long as they can continue to produce. Those in or near large inner cities will feel the effects most greatly, particularly food shortages and crime.

As extreme as this prediction is, if it is correct, it may well begin within a year. If it does, it will be wise to be prepared to act as soon as possible for self-preservation.

There will be three factors that will be key to self-protection in such conditions:

1. Become as liquid as possible.
2. Keep your money in a form that will not inflate, such as precious metals, and in a location in which it will not be taken away by collapsing governments.
3. Prepare a geographical location to escape to that is as unlikely to be affected as possible.

In Kansas, when there is a twister on the horizon, the family goes down into the storm cellar. Unfortunately, in disastrous economic times, the storm on the horizon is invisible, so it is human nature to hesitate.

Storm's a-comin'. If you do not have the three preparations above taken care of now, it is already nearly too late. The reader would be well-advised to put these in place immediately to avoid losing what he has, and ending up as a casualty of the storm.

Courtesy of Jeff Thomas, International Man

15: THE CRASH OF 2012

Our comment: While Jeff's conclusion makes sense, except for the fact that, during the Great Depression, the "Plunge Protection Team" did not exist. The PPT, as they call it on CNBC, is a timed response from the Fed to step in when markets are about to break down. They buy millions of dollars worth with S&P 500 futures, in a matter of minutes. Where do they get the money? Simple: They print it, and they can continue to print as much as is needed to keep the American markets afloat (up to a point).

Supporting this, if John Williams, from Shadowstats, is right, and we start to experience hyper-inflation by 2014, then the markets will be further fueled by the additional "liquidity" injected into the system. Stocks and real estate historically rise during the first phase of hyper-inflation. Therefore, look for a rising stock market until mid-2014, then, perhaps, the "crash." My suggestion is to get out of the general stock market and real estate now. Place the proceeds into physical gold, silver, and precious metal stocks, especially silver miners. Precious metals do well in both deflationary and inflationary scenarios.

Our action: We have all precious metals and precious metal shares, and we spend most of our waking hours educating our clients, and investment club members, about the value of doing the same.

CHAPTER SIXTEEN

China's Secret Plan to Bankrupt Millions of Americans?

"A fool judges people by the presents they give him".

—Chinese Proverb

THE COMING BANKING HOLIDAY

Some "conspiracy-prone" clients ask us if there we believe there is a secret plan formulated between Washington and Beijing—a plan having to do with Washington massively printing the dollar and Beijing buying these dollars, thus forcing their currency (the yuan) down. By doing this, China could export its goods cheaply, and the US could inflate its massive debt.

Porter Stansberry believes—and states that he can prove with his research, beyond any reasonable doubt—that the Chinese government has now put into place a covert plan that will extract enormous sums of money from both the United States government and ordinary citizens like you and me.

This plan is designed to take trillions of dollars worth of assets and savings from Americans and deliver this wealth to our Chinese creditors, who have finally lost faith in the US dollar. I realize you may think I'm exaggerating. But I would simply like to show you the facts, via what's available as public record. Then, you can decide for yourself.

And I want to make one thing clear before I continue: I *don't* blame the Chinese for what they are doing. Not one bit. In fact, although I know this will sound very controversial and perhaps even unpatriotic, or "un-American," I want to make it clear that I would do the exact same thing if I were in their shoes.

Our own government has essentially backed the Chinese into a corner, and we have left them no choice[.] (I'll explain what I mean by this in a moment.) To implement this covert plan, the Chinese are taking a series of dramatic steps. Some of these steps have been announced publicly. Others remain secret—although we believe it's fairly easy to figure out what they are doing, if you pay close attention to what's happening in the financial markets.

As China's plan plays out, I believe we'll see a complete disruption in the US banking system. I expect we'll see a precipitous

16: CHINA'S SECRET PLAN TO BANKRUPT MILLIONS OF AMERICANS?

fall in the US stock market, and a major disturbance of the US mortgage and bond markets. This, in turn, will affect *everything* about our normal way of life.

Most Americans won't know what to do when the US government imposes a "bank holiday," forcing banks to close (and allow no withdrawals) for an extended period of time.

Most Americans won't know what to do when they can't get a loan for a car, a house, or even home improvements. They won't know what to do when prices for basic goods (like bread, gas and milk) doubles in a matter of weeks. And most Americans won't know what to do when their credit cards and ATM cards stop working...or when all government assistance (including Social Security and food stamps) is interrupted.

And here is one thing I know for sure: How you handle this Chinese scheme over the next few years will be one of the most important financial decisions you make. As I'll show you, you have several options. But the absolute worst thing you can do is nothing.

Of course, I understand human nature. So I realize most Americans will in fact do absolutely nothing. That's because right now, almost no one in the mainstream financial press is paying the least bit of attention to this situation. But that will change soon, I assure you.

So today, in this presentation, I'd like to walk you through exactly what is happening. Getting a grasp on this situation today will give you a tremendous financial edge over the next few years. To put this story together, I've made several trips to Hong Kong and the Chinese mainland. I have also spent well over $100,000 to send more than a dozen of my analysts and even a film crew to China to get a firsthand look at what is happening in China

THE COMING BANKING HOLIDAY

today. Again, my aim is to simply show you the facts, via what's available as public record. Then, you can make up your mind for yourself whether or not I'm full of hot air.

As for me, I am 100% certain this Chinese plan will have a greater impact on your wealth and your future over the next few years than the stock market, the bond market, and even real estate, taxes, or the upcoming Presidential elections. Let me get right to it and show you what is going on.... *We are trapped. And so are they....*

For many years now, it's been clear that China would soon be pulling the strings in the US financial system. After all, we the American people now owe the Chinese government nearly $1.5 TRILLION dollars. I know big numbers don't mean much to most people these days, but keep in mind that this tab is now hundreds of billions of dollars more than what the US government collects in both corporate and individual taxes each year. It's basically a sum we can never, ever hope to repay—at least, not by normal means.

Of course, the Chinese aren't stupid. They realize we are both trapped. The US is stuck with an enormous debt we can never realistically repay...and the Chinese are trapped with an outstanding loan they can neither get rid of, nor collect.

So the Chinese government is now taking a secretive and somewhat radical approach. They have recently put into place a covert plan to get back as much of their money as possible—*which will extract enormous sums from both the United States government, and ordinary citizens like you and me.* Via their "State Administration of Foreign Exchange" (SAFE), China is now engaged in a full-fledged "currency war" with the United States and the US dollar.

16: CHINA'S SECRET PLAN TO BANKRUPT MILLIONS OF AMERICANS?

The ultimate goal, as the Chinese have publicly stated, is to create a new dominant world currency, to dislodge the US dollar from its current reserve role. Doing so will enable the Chinese to get back as much of the $1.5 trillion dollars the US government has borrowed, as possible. And here's the most important part....

Understanding *how* the Chinese will execute this "currency war" over the next few years will likely mean the difference between the opportunity to make extraordinary sums of money, and potentially losing a fortune. You may not think a "currency war" matters much to you as an ordinary citizen. But I can assure you, this war will affect every American man, woman, and child, whether you like it or not. To show you what I mean, all you have to do is take a quick look at what happened during our nation's last currency war. It has many similarities to the currency war we are involved in right now.

Here's what I mean.... How we lost $600 Billion! Most Americans probably don't remember this, but our last big currency war took place in the 1960s. Back then, President Charles de Gaulle of France denounced the US government policy of printing overvalued US dollars, which allowed US companies to buy up European assets at artificially low prices, and devalued France's reserve holdings. So De Gaulle took action...

In 1965 he took $150 million of his country's dollar reserves, and redeemed the paper currency for US gold from Ft. Knox. De Gaulle even offered to send the French Navy to escort the gold back to France. Today this gold is worth about $12 billion. Keep in mind: This occurred during a time when foreign governments could redeem their paper dollars for gold...but US citizens could not. And France was not the only nation to do this.... Spain soon redeemed $60 million of US dollar reserves for gold. And many other nations followed suit. By March of 1968, gold was flow-ing out of the United States at an alarming rate. In fact... [i]t's estimated that during the 1960s and early 1970s, we essentially gave away about 2/3rds of our nation's gold reserves...around 400 million ounces...all because the US government was trying to defend the US dollar at a "fixed rate" of $35 per ounce of gold.

So we gave away 400 million ounces of gold and got $14 billion in exchange. Today, that same gold would be worth $620 billion...a 4,430% difference. Pretty stupid, right? In 1950, our US depositories held more gold than had ever been assembled in one place in world history (roughly 702 million ounces). But in order to manipulate our currency (by artificially pegging the value of the US dollar to gold at the low price of $35 per ounce), the US government was willing to give away *more than half of the country's gold,* which we'd spent decades accumulating.

I don't know about you, but I have to believe that when the history books are finally written, this chapter will go down as one of the most incompetent political blunders in our nation's history. Of course, as is typical, politicians managed to make a bad situation even worse....

On August 15, 1971, President Nixon went on live television before the most popular show in America (*Bonanza*) and announced a new plan: The US gold window would close effective immediately—and no nation or individual anywhere in the world would be allowed to exchange US dollars for gold. To add insult to injury, the President announced a10% surtax on ALL imports! Nixon pitched these moves as "patriotic," saying: "I am determined that the American dollar must never again be a hostage in the hands of international speculators." Of course, the real reason for the run on America's gold was money printing and deficits, but like most politicians, Nixon was never one to let the facts get in the way.

16: CHINA'S SECRET PLAN TO BANKRUPT MILLIONS OF AMERICANS?

Most Americans rejoiced, believing that an end to the flow of gold leaving the country and a 10% import levy would lead to more jobs, greater exports, and a booming economy. But of course, nearly the exact opposite occurred.... Within about three years, America was in its worst recession since WWII, with an oil crisis, skyrocketing unemployment, a 30% drop in the stock market, and soaring inflation. Millions of Americans got a lot poorer, practically overnight.

And that brings us to today.... Now, roughly 40 years later, the United States is in the middle of another currency war. But this time, our main adversary is not Europe, but China. And this time, the situation is far more serious. Our nation and our economy are already in an extremely fragile state. In the 1960s, the American economy was growing rapidly, with decades of expansion still to come.

Today, that's simply not the case. And I believe this new currency war with China could wreak absolute havoc on the lives of millions of ordinary Americans, much sooner than most people think. It is critical, over the next few years, for you to understand exactly what the Chinese are now doing, why they are doing it, and the near-certain outcome. So let me address that now.... 127,940%...the most important number in China.

For most of the 30 years since the start of the country's "Reform Era" in 1978, China has been selling (exporting) more goods than they've imported. And the way it works in China is simple: When a business earns dollars by selling overseas, it hands that money over to the People's Bank of China (or PBOC, the country's central bank), in exchange for Chinese currency (called either the "yuan" or the "renminbi") at a fixed rate.

There's nothing fair about this. The Chinese people do all the work, and the Chinese government keeps all of the money. But

235

that's the way it goes. So for the past 30 years, China has piled up a massive amount of US dollars and other foreign reserves. At first, the dollar inflow was small because trade between the two countries was tiny. In 1980, for example, China's foreign currency reserves stood at approximately $2.5 billion. But since then, the amount of foreign currency reserves held by the Chinese government has gone up nearly every year...and now stands at $3.2 TRILLION. That's a 127,940% increase! It's simply astonishing to look at the chart of the increase in currency reserves since the early 1980s....

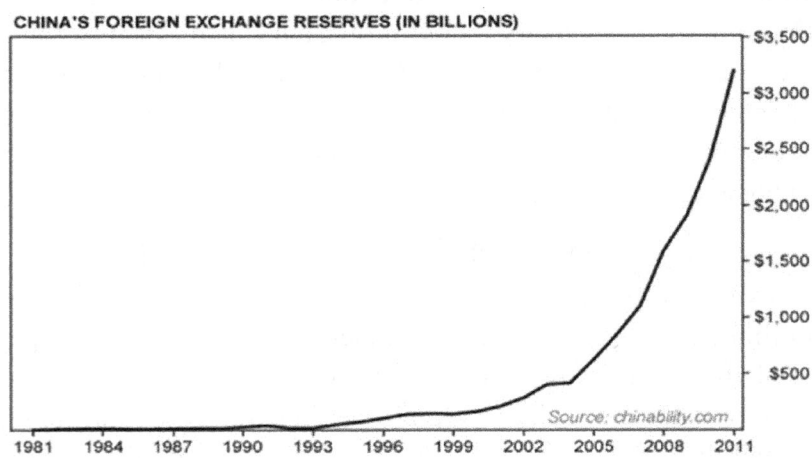

The group in China that manages these massive foreign reserves is called the State Administration of Foreign Exchange (SAFE). And for the past few years, SAFE has had one big problem: What to do with so much money?

What SAFE decided to do with most of these reserves is to buy US government securities (notes, bills, and bonds). As a result, the Chinese have now accumulated a massive pile of US government debt. In fact, about 2/3rds of China's reserves are believed to be invested in US Treasury bills, notes and bonds. The next biggest chunk is in the Euro. Of course, all of this money is ba-

16: CHINA'S SECRET PLAN TO BANKRUPT MILLIONS OF AMERICANS?

sically earning nothing to speak of in terms of interest because interest rates around the world are close to zero. And while the Chinese would love to diversify their holdings, and ditch a significant portion of their US dollar holdings, they are essentially stuck.

You see, if the Chinese starts selling large amounts of their US government bonds, it would push the value of those bonds (and their remaining holdings) way down. It would be like owning 10 houses on the same block in your neighborhood...and deciding to put five of these houses up for sale at the same time. Imagine how much that would depress the value of all the properties, with so much for sale at one time. One thing China tried to do in recent years was to speculate in the US stock market. But that did not go very well....

The Chinese government bought large amounts of US equities just before the market began to crash in late 2007. In fact, back then they purchased a nearly 10% stake in the Blackstone Group (an investment firm)...and a similar stake in Morgan Stanley. Blackstone's shares are down about 65% since the middle of 2007, and Morgan Stanley is down about 61% since the Chinese purchase. In other words, the Chinese got burned big time by the US equities markets, and they received a lot of heat back home. So they aren't real eager to return to the US stock market in a meaningful way.

That is why in China the US d0llar reserves just keep piling up. In fact, according to a statement by the government: "SAFE will never be a speculator. It mainly seeks to protect the safety of China's foreign exchange reserves and to ensure a stable investment return."

This essentially leaves just one investment, which can help the Chinese government grow their wealth, preserve their savings, and return to a position as the world's #1 super-power. The investment I'm talking about, of course, is gold. But why, exactly, do the Chinese want gold? And what do they plan to do with it? Understanding this is critical to successfully managing your money over the next few years, so let me explain the situation now....

China's Big Secret...Revealed

It was no surprise to us when, in 2011, China became the No. 1 buyer of gold in the world. For many people in the gold market, this was a big shock—India has always been the world's leading gold buyer. In India, people traditionally save and display their wealth in gold. Their entire financial culture is based on gold. Historically, silver has played the same role in China... but not anymore.

Of course, China is also producing the most gold in the world each year...by far. And every single ounce that gets produced in China—whether it's dug out of the ground by the government or a foreign company—must by law be sold directly back to the government. And here's the main reason:

I believe with 100% certainty that the Chinese are now clearly on a path to accumulate so much gold that one day soon they will be able to restore the convertibility of their currency into a precious metal... just as they were able to do a century ago when the country was on the silver standard. Back then, of course, China was a complete mess, looted and humiliated repeatedly by Russia, Japan, the British, and the United States. But today it is a very different story:

Now, China is the fastest growing country on Earth, with the largest cash reserves on the planet. And as befits a first-rate pow-

16: CHINA'S SECRET PLAN TO BANKRUPT MILLIONS OF AMERICANS?

er, China's currency is on the path to being backed by gold. China desperately wants to return to its status as one of the world's great powers...and they recognize the enormous power of having a dominant world currency. The Chinese know that in a time when nearly all governments around the globe are printing massive amounts of currency, backed by nothing but an empty promise, China can gain a huge advantage by backing their currency with a precious metal.

A century ago, China used silver to back their currency. Today, it appears they have chosen gold...and as a result, they are basically buying up the world's gold supply.* China is essentially now attempting to "corner" the gold market. As the great financial historian Richard Russell wrote recently: "China wants the renminbi to be backed with a huge percentage of gold, thereby making the renminbi the world's best and most trusted currency." Over the next few years, this is going to cause some assets to skyrocket, and others to plummet. It will cause some types of gold to become worth many times the price they fetch today... while other types of gold to become nearly worthless (I'll explain why in a minute).

Obviously this will have major implications for you and me. Now maybe you think I'm exaggerating when I say China is trying to "corner" the gold market. But take a look at a cable that was leaked by the US embassy in Beijing on the non-profit website Wikileaks last year. This cable was prepared by the US Embassy in Beijing, and was sent back to officials in Washington, DC. The embassy was reporting on a recent report about China's National Foreign Exchanges Administration. The cable quoted the China Administration as follows: "China's gold reserves have recently increased. Currently, the majority of its gold reserves have been located in the US and European countries. The US and Europe have always suppressed the rising price of gold.

They intend to weaken gold's function as an international reserve currency. They don't want to see other countries turning to gold reserves instead of the US dollar or Euro. Therefore, suppressing the price of gold is very beneficial for the US in maintaining the US dollar's role as the international reserve currency. China's increased gold reserves will thus act as a model and lead other countries towards reserving more gold. Large gold reserves are also beneficial in promoting the internationalization of the RMB [China's currency]." And of course, this is simply what the government is saying.... But remember: No government—or any savvy investor for that matter–wants to announce publicly what they are doing, not when they are in the middle of such a major investment play.

So instead of simply relying on what the Chinese government is saying, we think it is much more telling to look at what the government is doing. And here the evidence is overwhelming.... China's secret plan, in action.

You can see the Chinese government's covert gold plan in action if you take a careful look at three simple things:

1. The Chinese government's massive and secretive purchases of gold
2. Their "concealed" stakes in many foreign gold mining firms
3. And their ongoing changes to the international gold system

First, have a quick look at how the government is purchasing gold on the open market.... We can say with near[-]100% certainty that the Chinese government has been secretly purchasing massive amounts of gold in recent years. That's because we know for a fact, according to the most recent figures, that China produces more than 300 tons of gold a year—that's almost 50%

16: CHINA'S SECRET PLAN TO BANKRUPT MILLIONS OF AMERICANS?

more gold than Australia, the world's 2nd largest producer. And remember, by law, ALL of this of this gold must be sold directly to the Chinese government. No gold mined in China... not a single ounce...is allowed to leave the country. It all goes to the government's reserves.

Yes, the Chinese government allows foreign companies to enter China, and to form joint ventures with local Chinese firms. But even so: While foreign companies are free to mine as much gold as they want in China, every single ounce must be sold to the Chinese government, at current market prices. So the government is piling up every ounce that's mined in China... at least 9.6 million ounces a year (the equivalent of 300 tons). And that's just the beginning....

We can also say with near[-]100% certainty that China is also buying massive amounts of gold from the IMF and other sources, but keeping these purchases secret. We feel confident about saying this because this is exactly what the Chinese did back in 2009. If you remember, back then, China suddenly announced that its gold holdings had risen by 75%, because of secret purchases that took place between 2003 and 2009. These purchases moved China into 6th position on the list of countries with the most foreign gold reserves. But keep in mind, even with these giant purchases, China's gold holdings still account for less than 2% of their foreign reserves. That's a pittance when you compare it to places like the US and Germany, which hold roughly 70% of foreign reserves in gold.

In short, we believe China is at it again. In fact, on January 11th of this year, Bloomberg reported that mainland China bought 3.6 million ounces of gold from Hong Kong over the past few months...that's 483% more than during the same time the year before! This data, of course, comes from the Census and Statistics Department of the Hong Kong government. The Chinese government, on the other hand, does not make such information public. In fact, the Chinese have not announced their gold reserves since 2009. And when you look at the massive amounts of gold "disappearing" from the world markets, it's obvious that the Chinese must still be buying.

As Reuters recently suggested in an article that detailed the sale of 130 tons of gold to "unnamed" buyers: "among the most likely candidates is China, which has the largest currency reserves, at $3.2 trillion." When you are buying this much gold, it's almost impossible to keep the entire thing secret. That's why many stories of China's secretive purchases have been mentioned in the mainstream press.... For example, CNN Money interviewed Boris Schlossberg, director of currency research at Global Forex Trading, and reported that:

"China is considered a stealth buyer of gold.... As the world's largest producer of the metal, China often buys gold from its own mines and doesn't report those sales publicly. Analysts suspect the country is continuing to buy gold and could in fact, be the world's largest buyer consistently. It simply doesn't reveal it's pro-gold stance.... Announcing an aggressive gold buying spree is not in China's best interest because, for one, it might push gold prices higher. Secondly, it could devalue the US dollar, which would subsequently lessen the worth of the country's portfolio of US government bonds."

Forbes also quoted William Purpura, one of the world's leading authorities on the subject. Purpura is Chairman of the COMEX Governing Committee, and he said China makes it a practice to camouflage its gold purchases by not reporting them so as not to affect prices in the market. Forbes also ran a story recently that stated China could amass some 5,000 tons of gold over the

16: CHINA'S SECRET PLAN TO BANKRUPT MILLIONS OF AMERICANS?

next 5 years–about five times what they report as their official reserves today. I would not be surprised if China amasses double that amount. The thing to remember here is that if China is going to continue to purchase massive amounts of gold, the last thing they want to do is make this information public, until they really have to. The less they say, the cheaper the price they have to pay.

I interviewed Eric Sprott recently on this subject. Eric is a billionaire, and is probably one of the top 5 authorities in the world on precious metals. He has purchased several hundred million dollars worth of gold and silver in recent years for his firm, Sprott Resource Management. Here's what he told me: "I'm sure China's buying gold. I just have no doubt that it's the most logical thing in the world that they would be buying gold. They're seeing their value of their Treasuries declining almost every day now with the weakness of the US dollar. They are losing a lot of money, and they see the gold price essentially go up every day. Well, it's not a difficult decision to say, "Well, we should be buying gold and getting rid of dollars." That's got to be the easiest call in the world."

The point is, as my multimillionaire colleague Chris Weber wrote recently: "By consistently accumulating all the gold they produce, and most likely buying more in global markets on any dips, they [China] are saying much more than any official statement ever could." So that's one way China is trying to corner the gold markets... with massive and secretive government purchases of gold mined in China and elsewhere around the globe.

Here's the second thing the Chinese are doing.... ***Step #2: Quietly buying up massive amounts of gold in the ground.*** The Chinese government is now in the process of quietly buying up part or all of dozens of the best gold mining companies around the globe. The government basically has a slew of investments

243

in the gold markets, which it reveals as little information about, as possible. For example, very few investors realize is that the government's China National Gold Group Corp (CNGGC) owns about a 40% stake in China Gold Intl. Resources Corp (listed in Toronto: CGG). And over the past few years, between deals in the works and those completed, China Nat'l Gold Corp is spending over $1.1 billion in gold mining acquisitions, which includes the purchase of a Canadian company called Mundoro Mining, and several others.

Most investors also don't know that the China Investment Corporation, which manages about $1.5 trillion dollars worth of government money, has major stakes in some of the best mining companies in the world, including:

* Anglogold Ashanti: 100,000 shares

* Kinross Gold Corp: 250,000 shares

* Goldfields Ltd: 350,000 shares

* Teck Resources: 101 *million* shares

And it gets even more complicated....

China's biggest state-owned gold companies are fully acquiring and buying equity stakes in several dozen other gold mining firms. For example...

One of the biggest recent purchases was by the Chinese gov't-owned Shandong Gold Group (the 2nd biggest producer in China), which made an offer to purchase Jaguar Mining for $785 million in cash–that represented a 77% premium on Jaguar's stock price. Keep in mind: This is the biggest premium EVER paid for a large gold mining firm [as of May 2012, this acquisition seems unlikely]. Since then, they announced plans to pur-

16: CHINA'S SECRET PLAN TO BANKRUPT MILLIONS OF AMERICANS?

chase another gold company called Jinshi Mining. Then there's the state owned Zijin Mining Group (China's biggest gold producer by market value), which said it would spend as much as $1.6 billion a year on acquisitions. Last year, the company bought 17% of Australian gold miner Norton Gold Fields and a 60% stake in the gold company called Altynken LLC.

And keep in mind, the Chinese government, via Zijin, has already bought major stakes in a slew of gold mining companies in recent years, including:

* Long Province Resources

* Gold Eagle Mining

* Inter-Citic Gold

The point is, the Chinese government has quietly made dozens of gold acquisitions that we know about, and could have many more in place they haven't yet revealed. So that's the second way that China is trying to "corner" the gold market... by making very large purchases of hundreds of gold companies around the globe. What's interesting is that when you look at the gold China already has in reserve... and what they control that's still in the ground, the Chinese may already have more gold than any other nation on Earth.

And that brings me to the third thing the Chinese are doing to corner the gold market.... ***Step #3 How China will shake the gold markets in 2012.*** Right now, the Chinese government is reinventing both their own internal gold markets and also the international gold markets as well. Here's what I mean....

For decades, Chinese citizens were barred from owning physical gold under penalty of imprisonment. That lasted until 2002. Then, in September 2009, China became the only country in the

245

world that I know of to actively promote gold ownership to its citizens. In fact, the government started a major campaign to encourage all citizens to buy gold. Locals can now buy gold bars, which come in four sizes, at ANY Chinese bank in the entire country. If you don't think that's unusual, try buying gold at ANY bank in the United States, and watch the funny look you get from the teller. The government has also set up thousands of gold "stores" around the country, which look like jewelry stores, but instead sell bars of gold.

As *Forbes* recently reported at the scene of one such gold store: "The crowds surge shoulder to shoulder.... It's one dramatic example of the gold craze in China, which is officially and unofficially promoted by the Communist government." My friend Simon Black also visited one of these Chinese gold stores on a recent trip, and said: "On the inside, these gold stores look like jewelry shops–armed guards, glass viewing cases, etc. But instead of diamond crusted earrings and white star sapphires, you see bars. Lots of bars. "The government mints bars in sizes ranging from 5 grams to 1 kilogram. The prices are updated instantly ...and the bars are all serialized and .9999 purity, the same as you would get from Switzerland. "We went into several stores and saw Chinese people buying like crazy...all with cash...the inventory was flying off the shelf."

Why would the Chinese government do this? Well, China wants to control the world's gold markets. And if they can get Chinese citizens to purchase large amounts of gold in the coming years, it gives the government the potential for easy access to several hundred more tons. Remember, this is a Communist country. They could ask their citizens to sell all the gold to the government, or could even confiscate it if necessary.

You see, just like the United States, the Chinese government has a history of telling citizens how much gold they could own, and

16: CHINA'S SECRET PLAN TO BANKRUPT MILLIONS OF AMERICANS?

at what price. Here's a famous photograph from a 1949 issue of Life Magazine, of Chinese citizens rushing to exchange currency for gold. In an effort to promote confidence in their currency, the government offered citizens the chance to exchange currency for gold at a rate better than could be found on the black market, but had to quit the offer after just 21 hours because of the hysteria that ensued.

The point is, the Chinese government has turned their population into gold-crazed investors and savers. And they've taken further steps too. For example, recently, the Chinese made available the first yuan-denominated spot gold contract, called the Renminbi Kilobar Gold. As Dow Jones Marketwatch reports that analysts see it as "a step toward making the yuan global reserve currency."

But here's the thing.... Both of the developments I just mentioned may, at the end of the day, pale in comparison to the big move coming up later this year.... In June 2012, China has announced plans to open something called the Pan Asia Gold Exchange (PAGE). This is basically a direct competitor to the London Metals Exchange and the COMEX in New York. The way things work right now, the futures market in London "fixes" the spot price of gold each morning and afternoon, based on trading in London and on America's COMEX market. But both of these markets back gold contracts with only 10% of the actual metal. The new China PAGE market could have a much larger gold backing, and could forever change the way gold is traded.

As James Turk's GoldMoney site recently reported: "The potential effects cannot be underscored enough—PAGE is clearly preparing the world for a Chinese world reserve currency, and is doing this by bringing gold, and by extension silver, back into the Chinese economy."

Forbes also wrote about this development, and said: "It means the spot market in gold could be headed for China—and away from London's Metals Exchange or the COMEX in New York." This new gold exchange is a huge development—a big step towards backing China's currency with gold. Clearly, you can see that the Chinese government is determined to make gold a much bigger part of their financial system in the coming years. But where is all of this headed? And what does it mean for you and me right now and over the next few years?

Here is what you have to understand.... How China's Secret Gold Plan Will Affect You and me, it is now abundantly clear that China is accumulating so much gold for two simple purposes....

#1. First, they want to diversify as much of their foreign reserves as possible away from US dollars and other devalued currencies, which are backed by nothing but a foreign government promise.

#2. And second, China wants to establish a world-class currency, backed by as much gold as possible, which can eventually be integral to the world of international trade... and perhaps even become the world's top "reserve currency" one day soon.

This is going to affect me, and you, in two significant ways:

First, I think it's going to continue to drive gold prices higher... much higher in the years to come. And it's going to make some gold investments extremely lucrative over the next few years.

That's the good news. The bad news is that China's gold-backed currency is likely to help make the US dollar much less important in the world of international trade and finance. As Barron's reported last year, "China wants to establish the yuan as a reserve currency that could someday challenge the almighty buck." As the dollar loses its current "reserve currency" position, it's going to cause dramatic changes to our way of life here in America.

16: CHINA'S SECRET PLAN TO BANKRUPT MILLIONS OF AMERICANS?

Why? Because in the United States, for the past 50 years, we've been basically able to consume as much as we want without worrying about acquiring the money to pay for it. We've been able to do that because our dollars have been accepted and sought after, everywhere around the word. In short, for decades, because the US dollar has been the world's "reserve currency," we haven't had to produce or export anything to get all the dollars we needed to buy all the oil (and other goods) we need. All we had to do was borrow and print more money.

And boy did we. Take a look at this chart....

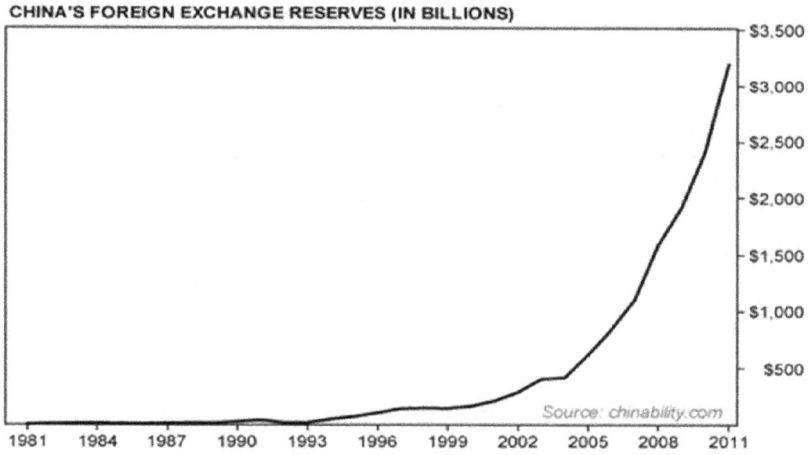

Even as late as the 1970s, America was the world's largest creditor. But by the mid-1980s we'd become a debtor to the world. And since the late 1990s we've been the world's LARGEST debtor. Today, our government owes more money to more people than anyone else in the history of the world. And that was before the financial crisis! Today we still borrow about $2 million every single minute, and we borrow 40% of ALL the money the federal government spends. With all of these bad debts piling up, we've had to begin repaying our debts by printing trillions of new dollars. And now, finally, the impact of this is being felt in a big way.

I believe our creditors (which include not only China but dozens of other foreign countries, plus other investors here and abroad) are likely to soon completely stop accepting US dollars in repayment...or greatly discount the value of these new dollars. What will that do to America? Well as other nations begin to prefer gold or even an alternative currency to the US dollar, it will basically wreak havoc on our entire society. And if we can't borrow money, banks will shut down. Government services will be disrupted and more likely, eliminated. No business, local government, or citizen will be able to get a loan at a reasonable rate. Everything we import...food, furniture, clothing, and oil, just to name a few, will get much, much more expensive. Our quality of life will plummet...in a matter of weeks.

As Sam Zell (one of the richest men in America) recently told CNBC: "My single biggest financial concern is the loss of the dollar as the reserve currency. I can't imagine anything more disastrous to our country. I'm hoping against hope that ain't gonna happen, but you're already seeing things in the markets that are suggesting that confidence in the dollar is waning. I think you could see a 25% reduction in the standard of living in this country if the US dollar was no longer the world's reserve currency. That's how valuable it is." Like I said, the Chinese are not stupid.

They understand the power of having a gold-backed currency, which could ultimately become the world's new reserve currency.

As a result, they're buying up as much of the world's gold as possible. The Chinese know that nearly every country around the globe is in massive debt...and nearly every country in debt is printing money (and thus, going deeper into debt), and debasing its currency. So the Chinese have come to the logical conclusion that gold is the *one thing* that can help them protect their current reserves, and perhaps even establish a true world currency,

16: CHINA'S SECRET PLAN TO BANKRUPT MILLIONS OF AMERICANS?

while almost every other currency gets printed to the point of worthlessness. That is why China is on a secret mission to corner as much of the world's gold market as possible. For several years, we've been warning about the loss of world reserve currency status for the US dollar.

With roughly half of our national debt held by foreigners, we have long believed efforts to print away our obligations will prove catastrophic for our dollar in its position as the world's leading reserve currency. But until recently, we were unsure of the exact mechanism by which the dollar would be replaced. Now, we see how it will likely unfold.... The Chinese will increasingly hedge their exposure to the dollar by becoming the world's leading gold investors. By taking over the world's gold markets and building a huge stockpile of gold, they would be able to back their currency with the world's traditional form of money. Once they are ready to make the yuan freely convertible, they will have created tremendous demand for their bonds and bills by making their currency the world's most reliable...and the only one backed with gold.

The impact on the dollar could be catastrophic. And every day the dollar falls, China's gold stockpile will grow more valuable (and more powerful). No, it is not possible to predict the future with 100% accuracy, but when people ask me "How will you know when to sell your gold?" I explain that I believe the end game for this gold bull market will likely be a situation where you can exchange gold for currency that is convertible into gold at some official price. I believe there's a very good chance that currency will one day be the Chinese yuan. No, it doesn't make me happy to say this. I feel very sorry for the millions of Americans who don't understand at all what is going on. These folks unfortunately are in for a rude awakening, and a big decline in their quality of life.

But it doesn't matter whether we like what's happening or not; it's just basic economics. China is going after all the gold it can. And clearly, gold is going to be much more important to the financial system—and much more valuable—in five years than it is today. Of course, here's the best part: Even if I'm completely wrong about the yuan becoming the next reserve currency, the simple fact is that China has more cash reserves than any country in the world. And China is on a mission to accumulate as much gold as possible over the next five to 10 years, which makes it very easy to position yourself to make money.

In other words, if you ignore this trend, you are ignoring what is probably the easiest, safest, and most reliable way to make money, and also protect your family from the inevitable financial crisis regarding the US dollar. For more information on this subject, visit the Stanberry Investment Research website at www.StansberryResearch.com.

Courtesy of Porter Stansberry, Stanberry Investment Advisory

LEGAL DISCLAIMER: This work is based on SEC filings, current events, interviews, corporate press releases, and what we've learned as financial journalists. It may contain errors, and you shouldn't make any investment decision based solely on what you read here. It's your money and your responsibility. Stansberry & Associates Investment Research expressly forbids its writers from having a financial interest in any security they recommend to our subscribers. And all Stansberry & Associates Investment Research (and affiliated companies), employees, and agents must wait 24 hours after an initial trade recommendation is published on the Internet, or 72 hours after a direct mail publication is sent, before acting on that recommendation. Stansberry & Associates Investment Research, LLC. 1217 Saint Paul Street, Baltimore MD 21202

16: CHINA'S SECRET PLAN TO BANKRUPT MILLIONS OF AMERICANS?

Our comment: It makes perfect sense. The Chinese now hold about $2.5 trillion of US debt, and this is growing. They can't precipitously start selling Treasuries and dollars in the FX market. If they do, they would certainly shoot themselves in the foot.

The most sensible way to get rid their dollars is to merely trade them quietly, for gold (and silver) and resource stocks. And what Porter left out: Start an "FX" program to buy the yuan, and sell the US dollar. You can't do this yet, but, as I understand it, the yuan will become a tradable currency in the near future. So what I have read here could be a road map to almost certain riches. The Chinese plan many years in advance, and they are slow to change their tactics, so get on board. My clients will be.

Our action: We intend to increase our paper silver purchases, doubling up as the price falls (no margin). When the yuan becomes tradable, we intend to take long-term "trend" positions.

SUMMARY

"No State shall enter into any Treaty, Alliance, or Confederation; grant Letters of Marque and Reprisal; coin Money; emit Bills of Credit; make any Thing but gold and silver Coin a Tender in Payment of Debts; pass any Bill of Attainder, ex post facto Law, or Law impairing the Obligation of Contracts, or grant any Title of Nobility."

—United States Constitution, excerpt from Article 1, Section 10

THE COMING BANKING HOLIDAY

When doing research on the expression "banking holiday," I came up empty. Not much has been written about this, with the exception of Gerald Celente's work. He covered the topic perfectly in his Winter *Trend's Journal.*

I really believe, as Gerald does, that there *will* be a banking holiday, and as you can see from the cover of this book, so does Joe Biden (or at least, he's discussed it). It makes perfect sense: The US has debt that can never be paid, at least in our lifetime. While the Fed *can* try to print their way out (inflate the debt), more—much more—must be done to show the world that the US is serious about its intention to live within its means. It can do this by raising taxes, cutting expenditures, and devaluing its currency overnight. I doubt if "the Powers that be" will do anything but the latter.

If you then, proceed with the assumption that there will be a *banking holiday*, or merely a slower type of devaluation, then it's paramount to protect yourself and your family *now*.

Motivation to Act

Many of the chapters in this book were inserted to motivate and inspire the reader about the seriousness of the situation. It is Monica's and my opinion that there really isn't a lot of time before capital controls are set in motion. Once this happens, Americans will not be able to get their assets overseas and out of harm's way.

Let Us Help You

The reader has it almost all laid out for him or her. Readers have us, who have spent the last three years here, making just about every

SUMMARY

mistake possible, and subsequently correcting them. Readers will not have to go through this trial-and-error routine. You now have us, who will answer your e-mails and provide you with guidance.

Get Your IRAs Overseas to Safety, or Cash Them In

We've made the move, opened our financial advisory business, and made a success of it, and we are now in the process of bringing over our clients. We now know how to get our clients' IRAs out of the country and into a safe gold and silver bullion Suisse depository (again, out of harm's way). It's certain that Uncle Sam will seriously try to convert all IRAs over to a lifetime government annuity paying 3% (when inflation is running at 11%). This revelation is huge. Up until I found out this legal angle, in most cases I was telling my clients to cash in their IRAs, take the penalty, pay the tax, and send the proceeds (which ended up halved) to the Suisse depository. Now, our clients can keep the IRA tax deferral going, with a full-bodied IRA, and *out of the US. Please call (727) 564-9416 or e-mail WallSt101@hotmail.com, for additional information on converting your IRA.*

Get Your Savings Account to NZ/Australia, Get Decent Interest, and Avoid the Probable Banking Holiday

Not only will the IRAs be safe (and, in all likelihood, spared), but readers can now open up a savings account in NZ, without having to jump in a plane, physically sign all the documentation, and showing proof that you are not a money-launderer. If you have the proper credentials, I will vouch for you, and get your account up and running in a matter of a few hours. The banks are safer here, and we use Australian banks for the most part. They are larger, safer, and pay a higher dividend than NZ banks. Interest for Australian one-month CDs (they call them "term deposits") is about 3¾%, versus about 3¼% in NZ. According to what I have read, at the end of 2012, the country of Australia will have little or no debt on its balance sheets. This is another reason to start a savings account in NZ, using Australian dollars.

I can't believe that any American would want to leave his or her life savings in an American bank, earning almost zero interest and facing a banking holiday (and/or capital controls). This move is a no-brainer. Let's discuss moving your investments.

Get Your Stocks to the NZ Custodian, or, at Least Do "Direct Stock Registration" in the US

Until the MF Global collapse, I had a tough time getting clients to transfer their investments to NZ using a custodian platform. Then Gerald Celente went on the air. He told the public that he felt the MF Global situation was an *"out and out fraud."* My job immediately became easy. I have, because of "MF," as Gerald calls them, hired a Kiwi assistant to help me open new investment accounts (here).

Prior to MF Global's fiasco, if any commodity or brokerage firm ran into trouble, *their* governing body would immediately rush to the aid of the investor and make them whole. When this failed to happen *this* time, and investors lost millions, the American investor became gun-shy. In the case of pure commodity traders, they became all but extinct. Why would you risk your capital, knowing that, if your firm became insolvent, you could lose everything? You wouldn't.

For those investors who decide to keep their securities in the US, it is strongly recommended that you employ "direct registration" of your shares. Get them in your name and out of the name of your brokerage firm. Even better, get the shares mailed to you, and place them in a safe place.

Don't Use an Overseas Bank; Use a Custodian Investment Firm

For investors who realize the value of buying, selling, and holding their investments overseas, I suggest you utilize a custodian investment firm, as discussed in Chapter Three. The custodian firm buys and sells any security in the world for you; it buys for you based on what you, or your overseas adviser, tells it. The security is then held in trust for you, in your name, until you wish to trade it, sell it, or wire funds back home to the US. To the best of my knowledge, there are only two investment custodian firms in NZ. Both are 100% safe. They are never allowed to have any liabilities and cannot take any risk whatsoever. And, of course, they cannot invest for their own account. They make money by charging a very small "custodian fee" of about .37 of 1% of your yearly account balance (virtually nothing). Your adviser usually charges 1¼% per year (much less than most advisers charge in the US).

No Capital Gains Tax in New Zealand

Here's the interesting part: There are no capital gains tax here. In other words, if you buy 100 shares of Apple for $625, and you sell them for $900, a few months later, there is no tax—period. Now, you must be careful not to trade excessively because, if you do, you could be subject to capital gains tax. As an adviser, shortly after the start of the new year, I send all my clients a computer printout listing all the "buys and sells" that took place during the year. You should give this report to your tax preparer, as the custodian will not; nor will they send the report to the IRS. Check with your tax professional about how to handle the capital gains issue. I personally report all my gains and losses to my tax preparer, and pay any taxes due. In summary, just follow the tax laws of the US, and you'll be fine.

The Investment Program that I Suggest (in New Zealand)

While I can and will buy virtually any stock on any stock exchange in the world for you, I usually follow a simple system that I call the "1/3." For example, a typical $30,000 investment account would:

- Have $10,000 of the funds placed in an overnight Australian dollar account. This is similar to our US money market accounts, but these accounts pay you 3½% interest per year, versus virtually zero interest in the US.

- Have $10,000 invested in three of the strongest mining stocks. The criteria: The miners must be "producers," must increase earnings, and preferably pay a dividend.

- Have $10,000 invested in gold and silver Exchange Traded Funds (GLD or SLV).

If the mining stocks were to fall in value by 25%, funds would be taken from the Australian overnight dollar account and used to buy depressed mining stocks. When the miners recover, some will be sold, and the Australian overnight dollar fund replenished.

Commissions on Stocks

If you could open an account with an NZ stockbroker (they call themselves "sharebrokers"), you would find their commissions rather high. Not only that, but the average sharebroker here would try to talk you into risky, long-term corporate or government bonds. However, we need them to purchase our securities. Now here's the good part: An adviser, placing an order for his or her clients, finds that the commission charged is extremely low. The reason is that commissions are pooled. In other words, clients each share in the cost of the commissions. This is a big plus!

Reporting

The US government, as every government does when it gets into financial trouble, wants to know where its citizens' dollars are. At the present time, reporting is easy and takes but a few minutes for each of the two forms. Form TD F 90-22.1 (the Febar form) has been around for years. You merely fill it out, sign it, and mail it back to the US Treasury department before June 30th of each year. The dollar figure used is the highest financial account balance during the previous tax year. File this form if you had a financial account $10,000 or greater during the previous year.

There is a new form for 2012 (submit in your 2011 tax returns): form 8938. It is a combined IRS and Treasury form. This form should be completed, signed, and enclosed with your tax return. Use this form if you have any financial asset, anywhere in the world, exceeding $50,000.

Always use these forms, as they are simple and will cost you nothing. If you fail to send these in, the penalties could be severe if enforced. This is a new area for the government, and it is expected to change each year, so stay tuned to my blog for the latest information at www.Banking-Holiday.com.

THE COMING BANKING HOLIDAY

Get Your Gold Safely Overseas in Switzerland; Store Your Silver Under "the Old Oak Tree"

For years, when gold was selling in the $400–600 area, I advised my clients to call ICA, a major bullion dealer located in Durango, Colorado. I mentioned that they should continuously purchase gold coins, on every "dip." I recommended that they *not* store these coins in their bank's safety deposit boxes, for fear of a banking holiday. When a banking holiday takes place, coins and cash may be confiscated. Depositories, on the other hand, are safe and inexpensive. I suggested that they be used.

I also advised clients to purchase *silver Maple Leafs*, bury them in the back yard, and not tell a soul. Burying silver Maple Leafs are still fine, and it would appear that the government would not confiscate silver. However, with capital controls right around the corner, and a banking holiday close by, there is a good possibility that *gold* will be confiscated. FDR did this in 1930. He confiscated all gold coins that were not considered collectibles, and then raised the value of gold by 40%. What this did, in effect, was to "de-value" the US dollar by 40% overnight. (US citizens saw prices rise by 40% the next week.) Could the government repeat this? Desperate governments do desperate things. Why take a chance?

Get Your Gold Over to a Suisse Depository (Before Capital Controls)

Switzerland is still the safest country in the world (financially), and the Suisse depositories are equally as safe and very inexpensive. The cost to store your small gold bars or coins is less than 1% per year—about .7% of 1% to be exact. The cost to buy small gold bars is only about 2–3%, over spot (very inexpensive).

SUMMARY

There are many bullion depositories in Europe; unfortunately, they are located within banks. Needless to say, it behooves us to stay as far away from banks as we can these days. There is only one depository that does business exclusively "in" Switzerland, and that is Global Gold. This is why I choose Global Gold for my clients. I have been actively moving my clients' gold from the large US Delaware Depository to Global Gold. *For further information, or to enroll in the program, please call: (727) 564-9416, or email: WallSt101@hotmail.com.*

New clients need only complete a simple application. I review it and then forward it to Global Gold for approval. Clients wire the funds into Global Gold, and I start buying their gold bullion on market "dips."

By doing this, if there is an overnight confiscation of gold coins, any bullion stored outside of the US would, in all likelihood, be exempted. You can assume that if the government confiscates gold in the US, the government will "peg" the price much higher, and use it (and other commodities) to back a new currency. If this were to occur and you had your gold in Global Gold, it stands to reason that you could sell that gold for a hefty profit.

Capital Controls

Just about every country, when it gets into serious debt, institutes some form of capital controls. At the first sign of a currency problem, the country's citizens start to send their dollars overseas or buy gold. This is one of the reasons why gold has reached such heights. This happened to Argentina in 2001, and it imposed capital controls quickly. This appears to be happening to Argentina again, as its inflation rate (the true rate) has recently exceeded 12% again. Argentina, as of late 2011, is forcing all foreign companies to exchange their profits to the Argentinean peso before bringing the funds home (to the US).

Can it happen to America? Definitely. According to John Williams of ShadowStats, US inflation is now running at about 11%, and we will in all likelihood have hyper-flation before 2014 (that's less than two years away). You will not be given any warning about capital controls; it will happen overnight, much like a banking holiday.

Therefore, as Simon Black states (paraphrased), get your dollars overseas now. You can always bring them back, but not vice versa.

Immigrate to New Zealand?

It's not easy if you are over 55, as you cannot work for a NZ company. Therefore those over 55 have to start their own business. Not just start a business, but have experience in that business. If you do, then you must submit your business plan to immigration, with the hope that it will be approved. If it is, then you are granted a three-year entrepreneurial visa (to get your business up and running). At the end of two years, you can apply for permanent residency.

If you are under 55, you can come over on a visitor's visa, apply for a job, and then, after a few years, apply for residency.

Google the NZ immigration website for complete details on immigrating to NZ. That all said, most will want to stay in America and just get their assets disbursed overseas. I think this is a prudent thing to do at this stage of the US financial mess, but if it gets any worse, and you want "out," then just come over on a visitor's visa. You can extend this for nine months and start one of the processes. Remember: Monica and I will be here as your liaisons.

SUMMARY

A final thought: When lived in the US we thought it virtually impossible to open a bank account overseas. This was reserved for millionaires, or billionaires—certainly not the middle class, having $25,000 to $500,000 in savings and investments. Besides, how would one do this? Try to open a bank account at a NZ bank that you never heard of? Let's say you did manage to get through the bank's "anti-money-laundering" third degree, and you ended up with a bank account. What we found out, when we arrived, is that *you don't want a bank account: You want a custodian investment account.* As strong as NZ and Australian banks are, it's safer to just have your money in an overnight Australian dollar account, earning about 4% yearly, as I write this. Australia has perhaps the strongest currency in the world due to its abundant natural resources, and zero national debt (as of the end of 2011). On a side note, if the Australian dollar rises faster than the US dollar (which most experts predict), then the investor receives the benefit. For example, if the Australian dollar rises 10% against the US dollar in the next 12 months, then the conservative investor would receive a 13½% total return during the period.

Our Free Newsletter

Be sure to sign up for my complimentary weekly newsletter discussing natural resources stocks, as well as providing links to interesting videos and audios. E-mail me at John@Banking-Holiday.com.

CONCLUSION

If you have read this book in a hardcover or Kindle edition, or listened to the audio version, you might have concluded:

- The huge US debt situation is bad, and getting worse every day. Once the European debt situation is temporarily put to bed, "they" will, undoubtedly, come after the US.

- The US dollar will start to fall precipitously.

- Those having IRAs and 401Ks will be forced to accept a government annuity paying 3%, when inflation will, in all likelihood, be running at 20%. At first, it will be thought to be voluntary, then *mandatory* (after an "event").

- Gold will continue its ascent to $3,000 and beyond.

- Hyper-inflation will set in.

- Capital controls will be set in motion.

- A banking holiday will be declared.

- A new IMF currency will be introduced to Americans, which will substantially reduce the net worth of millions of Americans overnight.

In conclusion, please give what the experts and I wrote in book some serious thought. If you concur with our reasoning, then start to take baby steps toward diversifying your savings and investments overseas. If your bank CD account is $25,000, send half; if your brokerage account is $50,000, sell out and wire $30,000. And if you have an IRA over $50,000, by all means get it completely into gold bars, over at Global Gold, now—*before* the IRS closes the loop-hole (and you know they will).

One last thing, and it is important: I am not a gambler or risk-taker. It is my opinion that anyone leaving their savings, investments, and gold in the US is risking their nest egg. Most would say that diversifying investments outside the US is taking a risk, but in actuality it's the other way around. I was a fair student at Georgetown, but I excelled in philosophy, especially logic. Logic, in my opinion, dictates here, to move at least part of your resources out of harm's way. This is why we wrote the book: to get Americans to wake up to the dangers ahead.

Thanks for taking time to read (or listen to) our book. Monica and I will do our best to answer your e-mails, and assist you in getting your savings and investments here, while we still can.

John and Monica
May 2012

www.ingramcontent.com/pod-product-compliance
Lightning Source LLC
Chambersburg PA
CBHW061633040426
42446CB00010B/1401